SABER ORDER

By Sabena Burnett

Copyright Sabena Burnett © 2017

Cover Illustration by Marc Burnett © 2017

All rights reserved.

ISBN-10 – 1546758100

ISBN-13 – 978-1546758105

CHAPTER ONE
Nan and Charlie

I expect they got on each other's tits from time to time, but being in their company was like audience participation in a music hall double act. Their constant banter was a contest of wits. Charlie was the most eloquent, and the better read, but he was by no means always the victor. He was a verbal artist whose rhetoric painted vivid pictures with words. Nan won her bouts with straight talking, and with concise and quick retorts.

She used to throw wonderful parties in the small upstairs flat, usually for the 'golden horde' – my Dad's name for her vast family, who came from far and wide to drink ceaseless crates of Guinness, among other things. I still have trouble remembering who was who. So did she – "Pass the rolling pin Be–Jean–Bert–Susan–err, Bena."

She was right the first time. My name was often shortened to Bena, or just Be. Nan had several different names according to who was addressing her – Nance, Doll or Ada, to name but a few, although her real name was Annie-Maud. Or Annie Maud Marya Bellsize Barton, as Charlie used to call her, for no particular reason, if anyone mentioned her real name.

But Charlie, well. Charlie was always Charlie, even to his granddaughters, except when he was naughty and then he was 'yer grandfather'. Charlie's descriptions of the inhabitants of Edison Road, or as he called it 'Widow's Walk', were vivid (and ironic, because Nan was probably the last in a line of widows, before it became fashionable and rich families bought whole houses to themselves, or as part as a portfolio). The descriptions were also very accurate, as in 'Mrs Here's Me Tits Me Arse Comes Later', not to mention 'Not Them Old Tits Again', or 'Her Over The Road With The Dopey Daughter'. There was also, inexplicably, 'Mrs Ginocky Trowbag' – this was somehow onomatopoeic, although I believe she was of Italian extraction so it may have been a cockney pronunciation of 'gnocchi'.

He often, with some relish, gave us a glimpse of the life of the old girl whose spirit guide was 'White Feather'. Any reference to her often gave rise to a whole running commentary of what the pair of them were doing and why. I don't think he was necessarily a disbeliever so much as he just liked taking the piss, and his understanding of Native Americans and empathy for their cause was second to none, due to his expertise on the Wild West (itself unusual for the time).

Charlie read a lot and was offered a job as a consultant on the subject of the Wild West by some library or another. He turned down the offer, as he was a proud working class man who did not want a white collar job.

"Wardy!" (I never knew her first name) Nan would shout vaguely at the inhabitant of the shambolic shithole downstairs. A warning that we were about to take the plunge to the coal bunker in the tiny backyard, and wade through the collection of furniture, clothes, and other items of pointless rubbish packed around several cages containing noisy birds. She wasn't in, but the door was never locked. Charlie used to say if a burglar got in they'd clear up a bit and leave her something nice behind. He had a point. Even her fashion sense was painful to the eye – a selection of grubby overalls and pinafores on top of a dress with dribble down it, and a torn cardigan on top. It seemed more like a road accident than an outfit (mind you it was cold in Mrs Wards') – it was a cacophony of different patterns and colours, like someone had thrown up over a Jackson Pollock. This did not make me like her any less, as she was a warm soul, who always had an interesting story to tell you.

Nan's flat was quite posh in the scheme of things – an inside lav, a bathroom with an unused sink (it was too cold to wash in there unless you were in the bath, and then why would you?). The hot water spat angrily out of a 1930's geyser above the bath, like a fire and brimstone sermon – slow and venomous. When Charlie worked on the coal cart, he would be black with coal dust coming home and be sent upstairs to bathe (sometimes Nan would scrub him clean with 'Omo').

On this occasion I now speak on, he was trusted with his own ablutions. Of course, he was pissed and the bathroom was freezing, so he filled the bath and splashed water about with his hands. She came upstairs to make sure he got in the bath, and he was so shocked at being caught out he jumped in the bath with all his clothes on.

The small kitchen contained too much furniture, as it was the living room as well. The coal fire in the front room was only lit for special occasions, like one of her parties, so they lived in the kitchen.

Charlie rarely moved from his position, perched on a small brown stool on the right hand side, leaning over the fireplace with his Guinness on the hearth. It was as if the fire had him under its spell, preventing him from moving away (so when he was pissed he often charred himself slightly). Nan always seemed to be making pastry on the pull-down piece of the 1950's cabinet, and he was always in the way – "Geddout the way and stop swearing in front of the kids, yer silly old bastard." Her being clumsy and slapping pastry about, he would invariably leave the flat with bits of pastry and flour in his hair, which no-one ever seemed to notice. If he belched she would pipe up, "I should say 'manners' if I were you."

In the voice of one of Wardy's birds he'd squawk the repeated, "Manners if I were you!"

Nan often watched wrestling on the black and white telly in the corner by the sink. She would jump around the room yelling "Garn 'it 'im!" – starting off by the fire and ending up dangerously close to falling in the sink.

One day, I was growing impatient at having been promised to be taken for one of our walks. She had only popped to the shops by the clock tower and had been gone ages.

"Where's Nan?" I asked Charlie irritably. Sensing my impatience, he said, "Oh, I expect she's got her hooter stuck under some old girl's bonnet!"

She was taller than most, and often three or four old girls would stand around on street corners putting the world to rights.

We would walk for miles up and down hills, arriving at some distant relative's just in time for tea. I liked Auntie Tinny's house. My teetotal Nan, who didn't drink it, probably didn't realise elderberry wine was alcoholic – strongly alcoholic – but very nice with homemade scones and homemade jam even so. We always came away with a jar of something or other. There was one relation that lived so far out in the country we had to take a bus (Essex I think), where I could see cows and sheep out of the window (I had not seen them close up), and there was an Aunty somebody-or-other, who lived by the pub (the Favourite) and had a cracked toilet seat. But my favourite place to visit was Auntie Doll's.

She and her family (and their families) lived in a big house in Hornsey Rise. We would have to escape the fangs of the devil dog before going in. This involved Nan shouting "Oo-oo!" until someone came out to say the dog had been chained up. Actually my Dad was more afraid of it than I was (this was because he had lived for a while in a children's home that had two dangerous guard dogs, and if the kids were naughty, they would threaten to set the dogs on them – no wonder he was scared of them).

Aunt Doll was a large gregarious lady whose entire ambition in life was to spoil the children in the family. She had been brought up in a home herself (and I always thought of mixed lineage, somewhere along the line, although this has never much been spoken about by the family – I think it was just accepted, but mentioning race at the time was probably contentious). Nan and Auntie Doll were partners in crime where colloquial nagging was concerned. Nan's best piece of work was, "Eat up your ice cream, before it gets cold!"

Aunt Dolls' was, "Them 'ippies wiv all their long 'air and beads!"

"Yes!" said Nan.

"And all that marryjooana," Aunt Doll replied. "They'll marry anybody!"

Then there was the innocent remark – "Everybody's been ill lately. I've been under the Doctor and Uncle Bert's queer!" (For younger people, 'queer' was an insulting word for gay).

She and Uncle Bert (Nan's brother, also cuddly and sharp-witted) lived on the ground floor – just as well too, as she could barely walk. Jean and Jack lived on the next floor. They were also large gregarious people, and their flat was always noisy and full of life. In fact, their son Stephen was also gregarious and large when he was young (not helped by Aunt Doll stuffing him with sweets no doubt). However, he soon blossomed into a slim handsome man, and as far as I know has remained so. Stephen always had loads of toys to play with, which was great fun. On the next floor were Aunty Peggy, Uncle Bob, Susan and Robert (it never occurred to me he was named after his Dad, as he was always, and still is, Robert). Aunty Peggy was a clever, energetic lady with a wicked sense of humour. Bob was quieter, when he was there. Peggy, Bob, Jean and Jack all worked long, unsociable hours (Uncle Jack was usually asleep in the daytime, as he worked nights, so we had to be quiet). I was allowed to wander up and down the stairs freely, playing with whoever I wished to. It was great! Cousin Susan and I used to teach the oldies the twist at Nan's parties.

Most of Crouch End's immigrants, by that time, were Irish or Jamaican. When we were on our way to visit some relation or other Nan would point out houses where black people lived, explaining that they were the houses painted bright colours (often yellow, orange, or bright greens and reds). Although there was some substance to this observation, the truth was my Nan was closer to the black community than it was pertinent for her to shout about at the time. I'm sure the so-called Christians 'passed a remark' (as Nan would say) about me going up the street to play with Mrs James' kids, armed with a homemade apple pie. As if her generosity needed an excuse, Nan would say things like, "Well, poor woman, she's on her own..."

(This could have made it worse of course, reminding the idiots that she was not only black, but a single mum to boot). As for me going up to play with her kids, I didn't see the problem. Mrs James seemed happy to have me (her house was always full of kids anyway, most of whom were hers or related, grandchildren etc.), and I liked the company. She used to teach me Caribbean folk songs like 'Yellow Bird' and 'Brown Girl in the Ring' and spiritual tunes like 'Go Down Moses' and 'Joshua Fought The Battle of Jericho'.

Although I'm not religious, I sang both of these with a gospel choir in a Seventh Day Adventist church a long time later.

My excursions with Charlie were a lot more adventurous and usually came under the heading of 'Up the Park'. Don't get me wrong, we did often visit the swings at Waterlow Park, but a lot of the time we would be

'Up the Pub'. Charlie's local was the Railway – a small family pub full of lots of old fellas (many of them black, which I particularly noticed after we had moved to dreary old Teddington, which was boringly lacking in multicultural people), who were frequently slamming dominoes on tables defiantly and yelling across the bar to each other.

I loved pubs, and I still do. They are full of such interesting people. Charlie's best mate was Jamaican – in fact at his funeral there were apparently more black old fellas than family.

Even more exciting was 'The Favourite' where the 'Golden Horde' lived, nearer Holloway. Nan's sister Lillian used to live around there, although she thought herself to be a little posher than the others. Occasionally Charlie would see 'Lady Lil' in the street, usually when he was black with coal dust (not to mention full of beer). He would wait until she had walked past him far enough to think she had escaped, then at the top of his voice he would scream "Watcha Lil!" just to show her up. Nan did not have delusions of grandeur like her sister, although she had worked hard to live away from the rougher area she had been brought up in, to the slightly better Crouch End.

Occasionally during our excursions, ominous looking white men would turn up and talk business with Charlie and I was sent to be minded by somebody's mum. Some of these 'business associates' were related to Charlie and some were from other cockney Irish families. There was one family we knew well, who weren't related but who also worked for the Krays (one of the brothers – of one of these 'friends'! – employed my husband some years later – I believe 'letter writer' was his job title). It's my understanding that there was quite a bit of naughtiness going on at the time that is probably prudent not to mention, but I am nonetheless going to grass up George.

Some years before, Charlie had owned a Suffolk Punch called George (15 hands). He used to bring Charlie home on the back of the cart – the horse knew the way home even if Charlie didn't... mind you the horse was sober. George, Charlie and the cart made regular trips to Billingsgate fish market. It's right near the docks, which were busy then and smuggling was rife.

They would pick up fish and take them to the Chinese area of Whitechapel, where the laundries used to be. Inside the fish were drugs, presumably opium (whatever it was, it wasn't fucking legal). Sometimes we used to get taken in someone's car to other places. Quite regularly we visited some people who had a stall in the old Covent Garden market (I think they were Charlie's relatives too). When I was about eleven, I used to 'make myself useful' by helping them stock up the fruit and veg stall, for which I got pocket money I was not allowed to mention to anyone. It was great fun. I enjoyed learning a skill and they were impressed with my ability to lift. They taught me how to lift without hurting my back. One of the 'Uncles' was trying to teach me to fire a shotgun, early one morning when there was no-one about. I was a bit of a wuss and was terrified I would end up taken off by the Old Bill. Anyway, I was a terrible shot. I realised later it was not only a shotgun, but a sawn-off.

Nan reckoned I was a true cockney for being born in 'the Whittington', so-called as it had been high enough on a hill to hear the Bow Bells, therefore named Dick Whittington Hill (hence the statue, the legend & the hospital). When they went to register my birth, my Mum, who is slightly dyslexic, spelt Sabena with an E. Just as my Dad was going to suggest she might want to spell it with an I, not that he was bothered, the rude and haughty Registrar piped up, "You don't spell Sabena like that."

Mum took exception to this patronising woman trying to embarrass her, so she quipped, "I'll spell it how I bloody well like!" (or words to that effect).

Contrary to popular opinion, Mum was not 'up the duff'. Places to live were few and far between, and To Let signs still read 'No blacks, no Irish, no kids, no dogs' – not necessarily in that order. So when the woman next door to Nan offered them a place to live, they got married quickly and moved in. Living together outside of wedlock would have been frowned upon back then.

They met each other in a youth club. Mum was seventeen. Dad was twenty-two. Mum already knew Peter – he had been 'quite sweet' on Mum and asked her to be his girlfriend. "But he was not for me!" she explained. He accepted this and they ended up lifelong friends.

Peter introduced Mum to his friend who had just left the Air Force, and they soon became a couple. Dad introduced her to Nan and Charlie, who thought she was the dog's whatsnames and she ended up spending most of her time with them.

The flat was 'part furnished'. This consisted of a desk, a tiny dresser, space for preparing food, and a small cupboard in the bedroom for clothes. Mind you, the shared bathroom had a water heater, but not the flat, so they bought one to go above the sink and a gas cooker. Mum said, "We loved it, our first home!"

They bought two chairs and a small kitchen table, and someone gave them an old single bed, which they threw an old cover over and some cushions as a sofa. They got a two-bar fire as a wedding present, scrubbed and polished the floorboards and Nan found an old rug to put over them. Dad was running a bookstall at the time in any case, being a bit of a swot, so his few possessions were mostly books. They got some old floorboards and put bricks between them and bought a bed on the 'never, never'.

Mum said, "What a lovely home. It was cold but we were young and we did not care, we loved it."

They lived there for five years, by which time I was born, and when I was three, the landlady (a Jehovah's

Witness) decided she did not want a noisy child living there so she gave us a week's notice – very Christian (no doubt contributing to my Dad's dislike of religion). We lived for a year with Nan and Charlie, but it was a small flat for two generations, and Peter, who had since married Lily, found them a tiny attic flat in Avenue Road, where he was caretaker. The only thing I remember was the bright yellow ceiling, stylish for a time when the inside of most houses were such dull sombre colours.

Life was by no means easy for my Mum and Dad in the early days. By the time they moved back into Nan's, Mum was child-minding Shaun (Lily and Peter's son) so Lily could go to work. She had Shaun and I all day at Lily's. Feeding us both, doing all her washing (by hand of course) and housework, preparing veg for her evening meal (Dad and Peter were working long hours).

When they moved to the flat above Lily and Peter, there was no tap, so water had to be carried up two flights of stairs and taken down two flights to empty down the toilet when it was used, so we were drinking bathroom water. When Lily came home, she took me to Nan's at 6PM and worked all evening dressing windows in Uncle Geoffrey's in Stroud Green. Later she worked for Wilson's, a huge local department store in Crouch End, and later for Winston Clarke Studios in Soho.

Uncle Geoffrey's shop was next to the dairy in Stroud Green, where the milkmen kept their horses. I used to give the milkman's horse a lump of sugar when they delivered – of course before my time it housed a dairy herd and a proper dairy, not just a shop and depot. You can still see the old dairy pictures in Stroud Green and Hall's Drapery is now a Sainsbury's local. The shop was a mish-mash of huge rolls of materials, many of them different types of lace for curtains and fussy bits to put on the edges. There were cottons of every colour and Uncle Geoffrey was quietly spoken and calm, and used to give me chocolates. When you wished to purchase something the assistant would go up to the top of a sort of pyramid, with stairs on four sides, where a woman sat with an adding machine, in a cupboard, looking over the top of her half glasses. She would give the assistant the change for the customer.

There is not much about Avenue Road in Hampstead that I remember, apart from the sprawling back garden (and my Mum screaming out of a tiny window at the top when it was time to come in). Nonetheless, my mind always wanders to Bram. I remember Bram well and, despite the obvious social differences, Bram and I liked each other's company. Bram enjoyed my curiosity and I enjoyed his tales of an exotic and exciting world I had never seen, and Bram talked to me like he would talk to an adult. I remember thinking at the time he was worldly wise, but I had no idea he was the son of an African Chieftain who would return after his degree, to rule over a huge area of land and people in Africa. That said, money and status were not things I had much concept of and neither was racism.

I remember one afternoon when I was playing with some kids in the shared back garden when Bram appeared. "I'm just going to talk to Bram," I announced by way of excusing myself.

"I'm not allowed to talk to Bram," said one kid who was following me in his direction.

"Why not?" I asked, confused – after all, he was not a stranger.

"Because he is black," was the reply. Not really getting it, I touched Bram's cheek and said, "He's not really black, just a very dark brown!"

Bram just laughed, and assuming I had solved the insignificant but baffling objection by my observation, I never gave it a moment's thought until some years later. To me someone with dark skin was no different than someone with ginger hair or blue eyes. I think he also lived with a fella – I did not have much concept of homophobia either, I'm pleased to say.

We later moved to a bigger flat in Ravensdale Mansions in Crouch End, which had a spiral staircase in the middle of the living room and other extraordinary and artistic phenomena, including an old fashioned blue and white porcelain toilet which would be worth a fortune now. I think it was while we lived there that I met a Jewish woman who had been in Auschwitz, who described to me what it was like to be a potential victim of genocide (only because I wanted to know). It inspired me to write my first poem about the gas chamber. She said there was something that drew her back to see the museum later, a sort of compulsion. It made her very sad, and I asked, "What was the most shocking thing in the museum?"

She said, "It was not the gas chambers, where my family had all perished, or any of the photos of the atrocities. It was a room full of possessions – suitcases, glasses, shoes etcetera. The little ordinary, personal things that remind you that these were human beings. That was the most shocking!"

Eventually, having been to evening classes at Hornsey Art School, my Dad got himself a job at ABC Television as a freelance designer. Apparently someone asked him if he knew how to 'draw up' his set designs, so he said "Oh yes!" – although he hadn't a clue, but he was a quick learner and he watched people like Ashton Gorton and Peter le Page, and copied what they did.

Being immensely talented and ambitious, eventually he ended up being their boss and running the design, graphics, costume, make-up and scenic artist departments as vision controller, and winning a BAFTA award in the 1970's for 'The Rivals of Sherlock Holmes'.

Not bad for the working class cockney boy whose dad delivered coal and whose mum once cleaned the steps of a brothel.

CHAPTER TWO
Teddington

"Crash! Wallop! Kingsway! Teddington 5692."

This was Charlie's version of how we answered the phone, and indeed his was a good description of the chaotic racket that the family was given to create in the little cottage in 'nice quiet' Teddington. When Dad was offered a permanent position at Teddington Studio, and got fed up with a two hour journey to work (each way), he bought a little Fiat to commute from North London (I bet you couldn't fix the fan belt on the new 'retro' ones with a pair of my Mum's stockings), and when my Mum started working more hours, they had enough money for a mortgage to buy a house in Teddington, near the studios.

I didn't want to move to such a boring old middle class place after living in colourful, vibrant North London. Incidentally, I felt the same when we moved to Norfolk later in life, and although this has been my home for twenty-odd years there is still a bit of me that longs to be back in that buzzing energy.

I missed the noise, immediacy, mayhem, and diversity that is North London. So as soon as I left home I went back there. Despite my misgivings, the little cottage by a children's playground in 60's suburbia was idyllic. I shared a little bedroom with my sister. Although I know we fought as siblings do, I don't remember it that way, and although we don't see much of each other now we are still close. We started by sharing the property with several builders for a while. If you looked down, in the kitchen, there was just rubble, and if you looked up just sky, as there was no ceiling on the kitchen, or the bedroom above, or roof above that. However baffled our parents were by the disarray, we quite enjoyed it!

In an antique Welsh dresser in the middle room was an old glass. My Mum and Dad had bought a second hand gas fridge when they moved into their flat in Ravensdale Mansions in Crouch End (not as posh then as it is now, but heaven to them), off some bloke with, ironically, a cut glass accent. He chucked in six old but unmatched glasses which they used instead of the nice new Woolies ones, kept for best. At the time, they were absolutely on their uppers. All the rest had got broken, and this one rather pretty glass with a swirly stem that was left caught the eye of one of the builders, who also had an antique shop. My Mum took it out of the cupboard, so he could study it further. Immediately, he offered some ridiculous sum of money that would probably have saved them all sorts of grief in the old days (and eventually they did flog it to him, after some persuasion, but after the money changed hands, they got him to confess how much was really worth. Its real market value was even more surprising).

By now he was seated again with his head in his hands, which he shook from side to side as my Dad described the other antique Edwardian cut glasses, some of which were obviously much more sought after.

Needless to say, a lot of my parent's friends had something to do with the studio. This was the case with two of our four neighbours in the small suburban lane, Jack and Jane Robinson (Jane was a wardrobe mistress at what was still ABC TV – my Dad ended up being her boss) and Don and Caroline Leaver (he was a director that worked on The Avengers and Armchair Theatre with my Dad). Later, Caroline, for whatever reason, left with their four children and married a Mr Crabtree. Caroline was delightfully noisy, I will never forget her screaming "Fingers!" as she slammed the car doors. One of her girls always tottered about in her Mum's high heels, to the point where she bought her a pair in her own size. This probably saved her Mum a fortune in expensive shoes.

I don't know what happened to Jack and Jane, on the other hand, but they had the most awful time with the South African couple next door (actually *she* was South African, and he had escaped the Mau Mau uprising in Kenya), and they moved away because of the rows. I didn't think they were as racist as everyone said, but that may have been because I confused Marcus Aurelius (the name of their cat) with Marcus Garvey. Well, I was very young and I knew more about the latter at the time. I mixed with a lot of the kids of designers and directors, and knew my Dad's colleagues like uncles.

I presume it was the influence of one such colleague – Michael Minas (one of the designers in my Dad's department) that prompted him to book us a holiday in Cyprus, Michael's country of origin. I was sixteen when we went. It was just after the military coup, and six-day dictatorship, but before the democracy created in August 1974, so it was a time considerable unrest – especially in the Turkish North, where English tourists were not greeted with too much enthusiasm. My Dad was not shy about voicing his dislike of the junta's treatment of the Turkish people. So apart from my Dad getting out the car to talk to Turkish people in the walled city inside Nicosia and nearly getting us all shot, it was a splendid holiday. Later my Dad and some other people from the studio rescued some of Michael's family, who were intermarried (both Greek and Turkish) from where they were hiding in the Troodos Mountains by helicopter and brought them back to 'Blighty' while the troubles died down.

Anyway – back to Teddington. After a short and vague education in North London, I went to the 100 year old 'Miss Collis's School' in Teddington, which appeared to do very little more than establish what I should have learned in Islington, but nevertheless what I didn't know must still be my fault. I went to Kneller, a so-called 'Secondary Modern' in Twickenham. I was heartbroken! It wasn't so much because I failed the eleven plus and did not go to Thames Valley Grammar (my much brighter sister did though), but that was bad enough. It was for political reasons that I wanted to go to a new shiny 'comprehensive', which would have undoubtedly afforded me a better seat of learning. It turns out my education as one of the 'left behind' kids wasn't so bad.

In one history class we were asked to choose our own subject for an essay. I wrote thirteen pages on how Stalin was a worse fascist than Hitler. Not realising this was not a particularly shocking opinion at the time, I was called back after class. Naively I assumed the political content was the problem, but turned out the teacher loved the essay, but "It looked as though a drunk spider had fallen in a pot of ink and crawled across the page!"

Nowadays they would have suspected I was dyslexic and acted accordingly, but she kept me in after class once a week until I was able to write legibly! I think for all the right reasons, and for which I am eternally grateful. The only other interesting thing I remember at Kneller was being called into the office of the Headmistress, Miss Hotchin. No change there... I was always in trouble. She rattled on for about ten minutes about Hilary Brett (sixth year) and I (second year) being such friends, and did I think it was really a good idea. At first I thought she meant

I was the bad influence, then I 'fell in' and – not being one who is backwards in coming forwards – I said, "How dare you, you two faced old dyke – you think we are having a lesbian relationship. We are not, but it wouldn't be any business of yours if we were – you want to concentrate on your PE teachers who like staring at girls in their knickers."

And then I walked out. It was her lack of bollocks in saying what she meant that got my goat. Of course this was not the thing to say (or do) but I expect it was not taken further as my Dad backed me up and it was the bloody truth after all. I had a couple of other friends at school, but I think they decided I was a bit young for their clique, yet Hilary Brett was my favourite (even though her family were in the Liberal Party) because she was kind and a generous friend who was what she purported to be, without pretention!

I left Secondary Modern, and went to Hammersmith College to take O-levels. It was much more exciting than school, with pupils from all over proper London. There was all sorts going on, not seen in a provincial girls' school. Spliffs in the common room, not to mention the dregs left by the sacking of the alcoholic Headmaster from Holland Park Comprehensive. One of the casualties, sent to finish his education at Hammersmith, had such a bad smack habit he spent his time shoplifting jeans from Kensington Market. Not knowing this, I took the bus with him one lunchtime. When we got back, he was wearing three pairs of jeans and four shirts.

Another piece of Holland Park's wreckage ended up so pissed every day she could not stand up by lunchtime, and when the caretaker went to his shed, it was full of her empty gin bottles. Generally speaking, I did better at college than I did at school, and left with five O-levels. Apart from helping out at Covent Garden Market, the first job I had on a regular basis was as a 'Saturday Girl' at Clarke's Bakeries. Calyn, my sister, had a job in the Twickenham branch later on I think.

Anyway, I ended up in Richmond. I really liked it and although I was only fourteen at the time, I got to run the place for two weeks when my manageress Carol was away (when I was short staffed, the Area Manager, who had a soft spot for me, donned an overall we did not know he possessed and helped in the shop). I liked Carol. I'm sure she had all sorts of fiddles going, that's probably why she wanted me to take over, rather than an outsider. She knew even if I had understood what she was up to, I would not have grassed. Also unsurprisingly she always had all sorts of men in tow, and while I don't mean they had a shag in the back (at least not while I was there), it was obvious they were extracurricular.

I say unsurprisingly because she was a charismatic woman (whatever I thought of her fifties mode of dress) and quite bright, and her husband was a bit dreary!

Later on I ended up doing a similar job for ABC Bakeries. I worked for a charlatan called Ada who was more than a bit 'warm'. This shop also had a little cafe in the back where I first got a flair for catering. I was good at making sarnies and making the rubbish we sold look edible. I also got a flair for justice (I had been a proper student by then) and started a Union at the bakery (amalgamated to UNITE). The wages were way behind all the other shops because bakeries almost exclusively employed women. Of course, being a Union rep meant I could no longer take over when Ada wanted to go on holiday as it was illegal, although she had become a member, and benefited from the Union status of the shop. She didn't particularly like me anyway and was just waiting for another mug to come along and do her job for her while she sat on her arse drinking tea.

I ended up having a blazing row with Ada, who was not interested in whether things were fair or legal, and gave in my notice, pointing out that she needed to pay me a week's notice as well as what she owed me. I then walked out and took legal advice and rang Ada who told me to come back for my money next week. Not being very bright, Ada said she had given my wages to 'my friend' with no shoes (unbeknownst to Ada I was the only person in South West London I knew who walked about in the street all summer without shoes). So I told her she was talking bollocks and went to fetch a policeman – she called me back and gave me my money! What she didn't seem to take on board is that I was not yet sixteen and shouldn't have worked a full day either!

My Dad got promoted at ABC Television quite quickly. Sometimes he used to take me to the studios, which was thrilling for a little girl who wanted to act. He worked on 'Thank Your Lucky Stars' – a bit like 'Top of the Pops' – and I got to see singers like Dusty Springfield. He even managed to sneak me in briefly when the Beatles were playing. My Mum (who is also a talented artist) used to make paper flowers for a lot of his sets. When he retired from Thames they made a film about his career, which included one of his earliest sets. This was Cliff Richard, Marty Wilde and Dickie Pride singing 'Three Cool Cats' on an earlier pop programme called 'Oh Boy'.

He also worked on 'Opportunity Knocks'. He brought me in for a rehearsal (I was very young, maybe eleven) and I sat doing my best to be really quiet and good. Hughie Green (a minor celeb, not known for his patience) suddenly screamed, "Get that child out of my studio!"

My Dad said, "That's my daughter! If she goes, I go. That means you won't have a designer for this rubbish!"

Hughie Green apologised. I was very proud of my Dad sticking up for me like that!

I don't remember a time when I did not want to act, but I think the clincher was meeting Jean and Mike Hodges. Dad had been working with Mike, who is a director (now of

'Get Carter' fame) for a while, when they did a teleplay together called 'Suspect'. Jean played the lead, and I was a dead body discovered lying in a wood by 'policemen' and their dogs. I was terrified of dogs and it only my desire to be professional that stopped the dead body screaming and running away. Rachel Kempson had a cameo role (her daughter Vanessa was my idol at the time). I asked her for some advice about acting, and she said, "Be yourself!"

It was good advice, although I didn't understand it at the time (I was about twelve years old). When she was waiting on set, she seemed nervous, but as soon as the camera was on her, she came to life and was magnificent.

When I was very young we went to holiday camps, usually places like the Isle of Sheppey, with Nan and Charlie. That's when I first discovered I loved the limelight by singing songs in talent competitions as a child. It was also when I first heard this story – once my Nan had borrowed a swimsuit from Susan's Auntie Edie. It had pre-formed cups but Nan didn't put her boobs in them, leaving them dangling below. When she emerged from the changing rooms Charlie burst out laughing and shouted, "My old lady's got four tits!" He was no help!

Malta was my first trip abroad, and on an aeroplane. Not knowing anything about air sickness it came as a surprise to me, and my Dad, when I chucked up all over his new suit. Apart from this unfortunate incident, I was taken over by excitement of the prospect of exploring a hot and exotic country for the first time.

My Dad decided I was in love with Jean Hodges, Jean thought I was in love with Mike Hodges, and neither and both were probably true. It was acting I fell in love with and watching Jean acting was wonderful. Mike and Jean's place, where we stayed, was in a village called Birkirkara. The Bonnici family lived next door and they became lifelong family friends. I had never encountered another language but when Gracie asked her daughter Laura (pronounced Lara) to pass the oil I gave it to her. I had not realised she had said it in Maltese.

Although I've never been brilliant at languages being able to think in another language is a wonderful feeling and made me feel part of the local community in the short time I was there. My Dad was a bit of a celebrity in Malta as he worked for a British television company, so they interviewed him on Maltese television, expecting him to talk about his design department. It was the time of Mintoff in Malta. The Catholic Church had signs up everywhere telling people it was a 'mortal sin' to vote Labour, and before they could pull the plug on him Dad had said all the Maltese people should vote Labour and get rid of all the British (and American) military who were just exploiting the people of the island.

The shot of my Dad being strong-armed away from the camera is a wonderful political moment for which I am still very proud! I have never been back to Malta – places are never the same and I have fallen in love with Italy since, which probably has more of the qualities now that Malta had then.

My Dad and Mike liked Malta so much they used it as a location for a film called 'Pulp' they made together. It was a film about old movie stars with Michael Caine and Mickey Rooney (Malta at the time looked like the Italy of the Hollywood era). It was a box office success.

While I was in Malta there was an English bloke knocking about at the time who I took an instant dislike to. He seemed to think it was OK to be rude to me as I was only a child, and worse than that, a female child with an opinion. I suppose he was one of the 'seen and not heard' brigade. It turned out my instincts were right. He got caught trying to smuggle a load of dope in a red Rolls Royce. Not that I have a moral problem with that particularly, just his assumption that being posh and obvious was clever enough to fool the hoi polloi.

Laura was a little sheltered and from a good Catholic family. When we went to Valetta (two fourteen year olds on our own) I tried to explain, even though I did not know Malta well, that looking closely under the caps of American sailors in the red light district to see if one was 'Bobbie' (with whom she professed to be in love) was maybe a little dangerous. I also pointed out that he probably had a wife and kids back home, and when we had finished the coffee and pizza he bought us, he was going straight in the local brothel.

She was having none of it (you could marry at fourteen in Malta then), but fortunately before anything untoward happened Bobby got stationed somewhere else, and although she was upset she soon got over it. Mind you I need not be so smug – I was always trying to get in bed with her brother Charlie (that didn't work either), but my desires were less matrimonial.

In my teens I spent a lot of time in Richmond at the L'Auberge café (at the top of the bridge next to the old cinema, now a Nando's) and at the commune at Twickenham's Eel Pie Island. This was where I was introduced to various drugs, mainly cannabis (which my flatmates in Stoke Newington about five years later used to grow in a cupboard with a light bulb), and LSD. I took some acid at one time (not as strong as the mescaline I had taken a month earlier, when I had amazing and mind bending hallucinations), but I think it was more my state of mind that caused the bum trip.

I was in the L'Auberge café (in Richmond) and some geezer I was trying to get in the pants of gave me some orange sunshine. He was keen until he found out I was 'jailbait' and disappeared. Meanwhile my usual group of mates had disappeared to a place known locally as the hash gardens, down by the river. As I was about to catch up with them the Old Bill decided to raid the place, and stopped me walking out. They questioned me, but fortunately did not realise (or were not bothered) that I was completely off my tits (let alone only fourteen).

That made me nervous for a start. When I got to the hash gardens everyone I knew well had buggered off, and I was not very comfortable with the people left, who I did not know anywhere near as well. However they could see I was dead paranoid and knew I was very young so they put me on a bus home. When I got there I felt really bad and told my Mum and Dad I was tripping. Dad was just cross to start off with, but I sort of understood that, and then he sat with me talking to me all night, telling me how much they loved me. Mum came in later and made sure we were both OK. I know I owe my parents a lot, but this was one of the moments for which I am particularly grateful.

I never took acid again, although I did take quite an assortment of other drugs. Eel Pie Island was a bit wild for the time (and so was I, I suppose). They had squatted an old hotel and turned it into a hippy commune and 'Colonel Barefoot's Rock Garden', where I saw such bands as Free, Deep Purple and King Crimson. I had once or twice fallen foul of Colonel Barefoot's killer punch. They had no licence so they used to make this stuff out of scrumpy cider and other things and give it away, and the other things were hooch of various kinds.

I saw some great music and had some really wild times at a very young age. It gave me time to learn what was dangerous and what I was likely to survive, and although I certainly took many risks I was a quick learner. I suppose you call it growing up! Everyone smoked huge amounts of hash and grass, as it was grown in the grounds. The Old Bill were not very hot on that sort of thing then. Don't get me wrong, penalties were severe even for a blim, but they were either not familiar with what it looked or smelt like or did not think it was important, in comparison to other shit that was going down.

On certain hot summer days at 'The Island' everyone would take their clothes off and lounge about in the garden naked. The garden was right by the river and there would be pleasure boats going backwards and forwards, all the time, full of tourists. The ones nearest us would avert their eyes as if they had not noticed, as if they were looking at something else. The ones furthest away would jump up and down pointing and yelling, as if they could not be seen. Business doubled! A lot of inhabitants of 'The Island' I spent time talking to were sort of 'hippy gurus', and one was called Eddy. He would sit on the main bench in L'Auberge and talk about the universe. He was a scruffy article who didn't wash much (being quite severely physically disabled probably didn't help), but he had some intelligent things to say and he was nice company.

Then there was 'Queer Paul'! A nickname he liked better than I did. Even then, when it was in popular parlance, I would not have used it to describe a person, gay or otherwise. But I suppose it pays to advertise, and it made his more deviant sexual preferences seem naughtier (he like to watch – nothing to write home about these days). He used to invite men back to his caravan, and as I used to tag along after the pub anyway, enjoying his company as I did, we quite often used to share men. This kind of sexual behaviour was taboo at the time, although I was sixteen by then, I think?

Paul and I were good mates for a while. We started going to pop festivals together. I think the first one I went to was Stonehenge. At about the same time I went with a group of mates to see 'The Stones' at Hyde Park. This would have been 1969. In the evening we had tickets to see 'The Who' at the Royal Albert Hall. Fortunately I can remember some of both gigs (it would have been a shame not to have taken in any of two such mind blowing events), although I was completely off my trolley for the whole day. I was full of very strong speed. I had taken Purple Hearts before with some bikers. On that occasion, I rang my Mum and told her I was staying with my mate Sue from school (it was the days of 'press button B' phones).

She wasn't having any of it. She said wherever you are, it's a bloody long way away. I made some excuse to get off the phone, like we were just having tea or something, but I was actually in Brighton taking drugs with some hunky, sexy motorbike boys!

Anyway – these things we had in Hyde Park were Dexys' (as in 'Midnight Runners') so we all spent the entire day gabbling, but the music was stupendous! Two of the best bands ever, in one day. It was at about this time I started to collect the poetry I had been writing since I was little, and write some psychedelic material about my feelings at the time. It was fashionable, if a little esoteric. Eventually I got to perform a couple of poems on Channel Four for an educational programme. Later on I performed them at poetry evenings and folk clubs. All the time I was going into pubs and singing. There wasn't karaoke then but lots of working class pubs would have a spot where people got up and sang.

After some private drama lessons with a mate of my Dad's, I got involved with places like The Cockpit and later Unity Theatre! I started as an extra and with one liners ('The knock on the door in the second act') when I was about fourteen and gradually got more and more lines and more interesting characters. The Cockpit was a vibrant place run by arty do-gooders from the local authority. That's not a criticism, just a statement of fact. It was the most incredibly vibrant and exciting place to be. They were used to young actors (I was about fourteen when I started in a small part in Sweeney Todd). I did loads of stuff with the National Youth Theatre there. They ran workshops.

When I was up West one day after college (I was still only fifteen), I got chatting to these lads who were buskers in the pub. I was singing along to the songs on the jukebox, so they asked me if I wanted to come and do some busking in Marble Arch (singing but mainly 'bottling' – getting money off the punters). They were quite good, albeit a limited repertoire, in which 'Streets of London' worked best. We did quite well, but I only took a bit of pocket money as they were living in a hostel, and I was living with Mum and Dad. I enjoyed the experience. It gave me an insight into the real world (there were a lot of street people I got talking to) and a taste for street theatre.

I was also going to a lot of demos at the time, mostly anti-Vietnam (hanging off the Houses of Parliament screaming "Hey! Hey! LBJ! How many kids did you kill today?"), and I got arrested a couple of times. I joined the Communist Party briefly, whilst finding my political way. After all, I come from good stock and however naughty Charlie was, he was a proper Socialist, who was hurt in the battle of Cable Street because of his beliefs (and buried next to Karl Marx in Highgate Cemetery). He used to say, "If you are not part of the solution, you are part of the problem."

He used to quote Pastor Martin Niemoller –

"First they came for the Communists

And I did not speak out

Because I was not a Communist

Then they came for the Socialists

And I did not speak out

Because I was not a Socialist
Then they came for the trade unionists
And I did not speak out
Because I was not a trade unionist
Then they came for the Jews
And I did not speak out
Because I was not a Jew
Then they came for me
And there was no one left
To speak out for me..."

CHAPTER THREE
Paul Hanini, and Back to North London

Paul and I met at the Cockpit Theatre when I was sixteen. He was the drummer in the band that was doing the music for some energetic play that involved fifteen-foot human pyramids (in fact, one of their actors was injured falling off one). I had played a couple of small parts in 'The Good Person of Setzuan' and was by then in a very interesting and political play called 'The Bedbug' by Vladimir Mayakovsky. It was running the week after the one Paul was playing drums for. We went out for a while, enjoyed each other's company – and then ruined it by falling in love. After a while, we moved into a little flat in Stoke Newington together. I had pissed my Dad off big time, and in the middle of a row he told me to move out, so I had assumed this would please him. Wrong! (I had no idea at the time, but apparently he was so upset when I moved out he was in tears).

Being a daft teenager, I assumed when a parent says "I want you to move out!" that is what they mean. I chose to move when they were on holiday – thinking this would cause less 'ag', not realising it would make things worse.

Anyway, my parents liked Paul and soon got used to the idea that I had spread my wings. They nicknamed him Paul Hanini – it is a Maltese term of endearment meaning cute. They were spending a lot of time in Malta as by this time my Dad and Mike Hodges were there filming 'Pulp'. A while later, some woman from House & Garden came to interview my Dad (his talent by this time had come to the notice of the media glitterati). When she asked where his eldest daughter was, my Dad told her I was off shagging some rock drummer, so she wrote – "Mr Downing lives with his wife and two daughters, although one works mainly away from home..."

Although our flat was shabby it was in a wonderfully diverse area. Stoke Newington is an innovative, pulsating area of North London. It is a mainly Jewish manor (at the end of the street was a school for Rabbis), but nearby Newington Green is Turkish, a few streets away, and in proper Hackney there was a Caribbean and African influence. A linguistic expert could probably tell which street you came from, as according to the main ethnic influence. Stoke Newington was a place steeped in the thick of the vibrant, cosmopolitan chaos that is North London.

It was refreshing living in a place where people had a sense of belonging to each other, and I got on well with the Hasidic Jewish community (a little respect goes a long way). I got a temporary cleaning job with agency called 'Spick & Span'. It was run by a couple. He was Jewish, she was Arabic. Needless to say they did not share this information with each other's clients. My discretion enabled me to work for both lots. One day I might be eating couscous in a house in Camden with gold taps, the next I could be cleaning a house with tapestries all over the walls in Golders Green. The name was their idea of a joke – they had had so much shit about their mixed marriage, they explained, so loosely speaking, the term 'Spic' was a rude word for Jewish (strictly speaking Mexican, but also Jewish) and 'Span' was a slang term for Arabic (strictly speaking Indo-European, but used to mean anyone vaguely Arabic or 'swarthy').

Apart from the obvious, culturally, they were two of the most 'Gawd Blimey' cockneys you've ever met. I had a great time being spoiled by all their customers, especially at Ramadan and Passover, when they had to clear out all the food for fasting. Because I was a good worker they all wanted me to work for them and cut out the middle man – in this case Hymie. Rather than moonlighting, and fleecing the old couple out of their agency fees (income, no doubt hidden from the taxman), or working and signing on, like everyone else seemed to be in North London, I decided I needed a proper full-time job. Everyone in North London seemed to be 'at it', in some way or another, and assuring me it was was the only way to survive (more about that later, especially in Chapter Seven).

The first one that came up was in the roughest pub even I have ever worked in. The Silver Bullet lurks threateningly over Finsbury Park Station, like a large bouncer. The only women who had worked there before were 'Waitresses' and the place was still jam packed full of other 'Ladies of the Night' and their gentlemen, who were not only pimps, but most of them had another couple of additional lines of work (you know – selling smack, fencing, stabbing and shooting people for a living... that sort of thing).

I pretended to be naïve, so I was polite and treated customers with respect, but at the same time didn't take any shit off anyone, so we all got on fine. One time, while the others were busy sorting out a brawl, this twat tried to accost me outside the ladies' room, in between public areas. He asked me what would happen if he took me into the empty bar and fucked me. I answered his question quickly by contacting his nether regions with my boot, which saw him off.

The two resident bouncing barmen were from Belfast, one from the 'Falls' and one from the 'Shanklin'. They were, however, really protective of each other, and good mates, even though they had worked out they were probably trying to kill each other back home. This fact did not deter them from goading each other, as they got more pissed. This consisted of a competition to see who could sing the most murderous rebel song. This would culminate in the customary punch up after time, all forgotten by the next day of course. It was through them I ended up going out with a bouncer from the Clarendon (Hammersmith) who turned out to be a mercenary working for both sides, and on the run from them and the Old Bill (I wondered why he suddenly disappeared).

I worked in about fifty pubs altogether in London in the end, and many of them were quite rough, especially the ones up Holloway Road. Many of the Irish pubs, in the early days, were still paying dues to the IRA (in return publicans would often enjoy protection from a couple of enforcers), and there were a lot of Irish establishments in that part of London. Some of them were even brewery pubs. One such publican showed us a video given to him by the brewery showing, blatantly, that he was buying in his own booze but he had still managed to intimidate them out of prosecuting him. I later worked for his mates up the road, a lovely couple called Keith and Lesley, who were English. They had trained in the pub in Crouch End where I ended up training later.

The first time I was called upon to prove my strength (because I was a woman) was while I working for them at the Old King's Head, Holloway Road. By this time they'd got rid of their smelly barman. It was the only time I ever heard Lesley swear. We were upstairs sorting out the rota, when he passed the kitchen door on his way down to the bar, in clothes he had probably slept in. I was quite taken aback when she uttered under her breath with venom "He's got that fucking red jumper on again!"

I did a double-take at Lesley, as if checking someone else had not blurted out this sentence. Anyway the area manager (I found out afterwards) wanted to know from Keith how a mere woman could possibly cope with the cellar work. The main lager we sold was in full barrels (36 gallons) but the one in the back bar was nearly empty (we did not sell much in there). He told me to swap it with the one in the front bar (where we sold loads), which was full. After politely pointing out there was no logic to this, I said "You're the governor!" and swapped them over. It was a long bar but as I rolled the full barrel upright it took me less than two minutes, and they could hear me in the cellar as the pub was empty. The area manager was won over! When Keith bought his own pub I was upset that he did not take me with him. I found out much later when I went to visit them in their next pub in South London that the Aussie I was screwing at the time was thieving off him. They must have realised by this time I had not got a clue, because they welcomed me like an old friend. I had a drink over there a couple of times and took some mates down, to introduce them to the delights of life 'south of the border, down Woolwich way'!

A lot later I moved out of London, probably to Bristol, to do something or other theatrical, and we lost touch.

I went out with a villain later, I had known for a while, who was working as a barman in The Mother Redcap on the other end of Holloway Road (whilst 'resting' from his normal profession, which involved spending long spells at Her Majesty's pleasure). I did a few bar sessions there to help out. The geezer he was working for seemed to be trying to drink the place dry, on account of his missus running off with his last barman. He was so drunk one night we thought it best to stay upstairs with him in case he did himself an injury. This ended up like a bedroom farce with him trying to get in bed next to me (although his barman was in it with me, in his drunken head he must have thought I was up for some sort of threesome, rather than concerned for his welfare), and us swapping to his bed, and him following, etcetera. Eventually the dozy article put a bottle through his own pub window (don't ask me why) and tried to make out it was some lads walking past. The brewery got rid of him soon after. But I digress....

Living with Paul was exciting. We spent about the first three months in bed, and on the ground in the park and nearly in the car once when we drove home from a party and crashed. Oh, and once up against his bedroom wall at his parent's house (we were trying to be quiet), who overheard and muttered something about that sort of thing just being lust. Lust was OK with me. At first Paul used to write romantic poetry, in beautiful handwriting with illustrations. He was older than me (thirty two) and rushed around all over the place doing gigs. Some of which were brilliant, since he was in a lot of bands.

At one time he was with a soul band called Mossa. They played very some very rough gigs all over the country, and also a club called then called the Four Aces in Hackney. Paul was often the only white fella in the club (not that this was ever a problem). Other pure money making music he played was with an agency. One regular gig was with an old boy who plonked some sort of jazz on a piano at various insalubrious establishments in the East End, and sometimes south of the river. My favourites were the Queens Arms in Stockwell Road and the Vauxhall Tavern (a veritable den of iniquity, but all family so if the young ones were out of order Granddad would give them the gypsy warning).

This was where I ended up doing singer/compère work, you know – a few music hall songs, like 'I'm One of the Ruins that Cromwell Knocked About a Bit', 'Oh What a Beauty' (all of them filthy), and a bit of crooning. Eventually, and a lot later but still through this agency, I began to striptease at The Skinners Arms (up the Cross) and some other dive in South London. The Vauxhall Tavern became known as the up and coming place for drag, and I had some great drunken evenings with the very talented artistes who performed there.

Paul was also in a band with a nice bloke called Martin Lee for a while, who was also in two other bands, one being 'Brotherhood of Man'. We had been out with Martin and his missus a few times, and he used to come round the flat now and again, but we lost touch with him when he started getting famous. One day he came round and invited us to a Brotherhood of Man gig, although it was not my sort of thing. Martin had been like a kindly uncle to me when Paul and he were in a band, so I was not surprised at the invitation. At the gig we got VIP treatment and were drinking extortionately expensive champagne in the dressing room.

Martin asked me what I thought of the gig. Being a girl that speaks my mind I said it was not my sort of thing, although I was really impressed by the whole professional slickness of their performance – not like fringe theatre at all. I did not like the commercial aspect – for instance his new song 'Save All Your Kisses for Me' did not seem sincere, and more like the mushy stuff audiences wanted to hear. When he explained that it was really about his daughter, that he'd taken up with this lovely girl in the band and his wife had stopped him seeing his daughter, I ended up in tears. The song was about missing her. I was so embarrassed – the hotheadedness, impetuosity and arrogance of youth, eh?

While I was living with Paul I auditioned for loads of drama schools, and I was promised a place in The Bristol

Old Vic to start the next year and Manchester University if I got one A Level. I was accepted at Mountview. Although my Dad did not want me to go to as he had worked with the principal and did not like him (not his exact description – I think the words 'fucking' and 'idiot' came into it), I knew he was probably right, but I was restless and impulsive so decided to go there.

Drama school was emotionally wrenching. They take you apart and put you back together again (some students did not mend well, and it all ended in real life tragedy). I liked all the students in my class including (now well-known) Glynis Barber (she was Glynis Van De Riet then and very South African, but enormously talented and confident), except her first husband Paul. As they say in Norfolk, I couldn't abide him.

I liked Siv Borg (as she now calls herself) but my favourite, and in my opinion the most talented, was Decima Francis (Dizzy). Dizzy was a fabulous singer, in fact when she auditioned for Dan at the Kings Head (see Chapter Four) I tried to persuade him to take her, but he had someone else in mind. I understand she's had a fabulous career, in any case.

Acting was definitely my favourite pastime by the time I went to Mountview, but even after I split with Paul, sex ran a close second. Unless you've got prudish ideas about ladies and gentlemen, you will agree, most students of either sex like playing the field, and spend a great deal of time getting the object of their desire between the sheets (or wherever). Women are sometimes maybe a little more subtle (not in my case), although equal contenders. I had many lovers who were also students. One of my lovers at drama school was a Scottish bloke called Billy Collins (not his acting name). He was in a whodunnit I was watching recently and is a splendid actor (he was a pretty hot lover as I remember as well). I was not looking for a long term relationship, but I did not sleep with anyone I was not fond of.

After drama school, I went on to work for the old Unity Theatre. I was in five plays there, including one about Indonesia (the title of which escapes me), which had a short run and starred Bob Hoskins. Like him I was recruited whilst drinking in the bar, but unlike him it was my intention to get involved. I also worked behind the ramp with a lovely bloke called Norman Beddows. Some journalist geezer was giving me a load of old chat – "First you're sweeping the floor, then you're behind the bar with Norman, then you're acting in the play, then you're flying scenery, then you are singing in the folk club... what exactly is your job round here?"

Norman said wryly, in his best cockney, "General dogsbody! Like the bloody rest of us mate!"

The reporter put it in his paper. Now I know people joked about Norman moaning, but he had a lot to contend with in keeping Unity going for posterity. He and a smashing fella called Ray Cross (who wrote most of the plays) were the life and soul of Unity. Ray was your archetypal actor at first glance, but there was a lot more to him than that, and apart from anything else he was amazingly talented and versatile. He had solid political and ambitious reasons to get involved with Unity (as we all did) and I am very proud to have been part of such an innovative and creative political movement. Alan Plater came to see us in the premier of his brilliant 'The Tigers Are Coming OK'. Amazingly, he thought my accent was accurate (I've still never been to Hull). I had this scene with a very gorgeous fella I was sleeping with at the time and we had to kiss passionately – all the clips used to fall out the back of my hair and I invariably got carried away and forgot my next line.

On the last night there was a scene where the Prime Minister meets someone in the Gents' (don't ask), and Ray Cross was the lead. We got two old jugs and poured water noisily from one to the other, behind the set, when they were supposed to be pissing. It was a childish joke and Ray was not amused but describes the feel of the atmosphere of fun that was about the place at the time, as if something exciting was about to happen!

After the last play I was in at Unity – 'Common Will, Against the Giant' (a commie panto), they had the big fire. One of the right wing neo-Nazi groups was suspected but I don't think it was ever proven.

I was constantly doing auditions. Apart from not being able to sight read I was nervous, with crippling stage fright and struggled to learn lines. But I nevertheless managed to do some good work in Theatre in Education and London Fringe. I started with Bristol Gate Theatre Company – mostly ex-students, from the University. We toured schools and arts centres all over the West Country, Wales and London, with Peer Gynt (which was on the GCE curriculum) and The Queen of the Snow. Both plays had some excellent moments of comedy and we had only a suggestion of costume and almost no sets as such. In the Queen of the Snow, a spoof on fairytales, we devised one of the simplest but effective bits of business. Two white sheets were attached to strips of wood, top and bottom, and held up in front of two actors each side of the stage, masking them and both sidestepped across the stage. As they crossed in the middle, the Snow Queen, who was behind one of them, stopped centre stage, seeming to appear from nowhere. It was so slick, like a magician's sleight of hand. There was always a gasp and sometimes a round of applause. The kids loved it!

Paul and I enjoyed quite a good little relationship, until it became obvious he was playing away. He had mentioned marriage early on, but I pointed out I was very young, although I was keen. Later he seemed to lose interest in the idea. This seemed to give him licence to mess about, and I was very hurt when I found out but decided to cut my losses and find some extracurricular activity of my own. After all, we had not made any promises, and there was a whole world of interesting, beautiful, sexy men out there. Eventually I confessed (he didn't, but he knew I knew), and we decided to call it a day.

I moved out, into a squat in Highbury. Well three houses of squat in Highbury to be precise. The place was well known at the time for its stance against slum landlords who sat on property, plus the neighbours liked us and we were in all the papers. One family who lived there were doing up an old sixties ambulance, which was the height of luxury inside by the time they moved into it. We have kept in touch after what must be at least forty years, and after their family grew up and they semi-retired and rented out their beautiful house in Hampshire, they are living in something similar (a modern camper van) and travelling around the world – back on the road again, as Canned Heat said!

Don't get me wrong, living in squats was not pleasant. Most of the residents of this particular one were in genuine need, improved the environment they lived in and treated the place and others who lived there with respect. Some of the twats in other places I squatted smashed the place up and lived in squalor. However, no-one would live in any squat if they had a choice. So I saved up for a deposit and eventually moved into a flat in Barnsbury. although I was only there a short time.

The landlord was a nice old Greek fella. The design of the dark basement was odd. The Landlord's office was in the centre, with a passageway each side of leading to the French windows and the garden. He often used to wander about downstairs between his office and the garden, muttering to himself. The door to said 'office' faced two doors at the front, one being my bedsit, and the other belonging to a middle-aged Irish bloke. Well, he used to collect the rent every Wednesday in the room upstairs (the only time me and the Irish geezer used the front door). He would be up there all morning collecting rent from various properties, so people would be in and out constantly.

One Wednesday when I came upstairs to pay my rent, the front door was locked. I couldn't stop as I was late for work. No-one came for the rent, but about two days later at roughly ten o'clock at night I heard a noise in the passageway. I opened the door and there was the landlord shuffling from the office down one of the passageways. "Excuse me," I called towards him. "You haven't got my rent for this week yet!"

I could never remember his name. He did not respond and wandered off along the passage where it was darker. I thought the fact that he was wandering around in the dark was odd at the time. Next day I bumped into the Irish fella. I explained that he had not taken my rent and that I had seen him last night and he had ignored me. The Irish fella said, "Don't be daft. You couldn't have seen him last night – he's been dead a week!"

One of the landlord's relations came for the rent eventually and told us we would need to leave as she was selling the place. She confirmed that he had died before rent day so, as I was wide awake and stone cold sober when the encounter occurred, I can only conclude I must have seen a ghost!

CHAPTER FOUR
The King's Head

By the time I had been at drama school for a while, I realised my Dad was right about the Principal and his band of followers. One of his sycophants stood up in class and started going off on one one day – "The Head of the School said that in *real* theatre…"

"Let me stop you there!" I interrupted angrily. "That bellend has not set foot inside a *real* theatre for the last thirteen years. I work in a *real* theatre…"

"How can you be working in a theatre while you are at drama school?" the dickhead said.

"How do you imagine I pay my fees, rich boy?"

I lived in the wrong London Borough to get help from the government. Surprisingly, the 'Socialist Republic of Islington' did not give Mountview students a grant. You had to be from Hornsey, Tottenham or Camden. For those of us whose parents were not on the 'Forbes' list, we were allowed to earn 'pocket money' by doing shifts at the student bar. I needed to find a way to pay my fees properly, but until then any earnings were welcome.

'The Bar Stewards' invented some lethal cocktails, named after whichever show that was playing that week. 'Blithe spirit' was bad enough, but 'Six Characters in

Search of an Author' created one or two casualties. I can't remember the exact recipe, but the 'Six Characters' included four spirits, two liqueurs and not much else!

One of its victims, who ended up in a chaotic heap on the floor of the bar, was the play's director, a senior tutor, who one of the students had to take home.

So I needed a proper part time job. I had £250 my Nan had given me (a lot of money in those days) and that was it. So Paul, the drummer, introduced me to Mike Khan. As Mike booked all the music for The King's Head, his band had top spot Friday, Saturday and Sunday nights, so he had a bit of clout with Dan Crawford – the guv'nor. So this started my on-off association with the Kings Head Pub and Theatre. I started as a part time waitress and box office assistant. Eventually I ended up behind the ramp as well as cooking the food and even running the place for two weeks (I was also Dan's occasional lover, although not exclusively – that was not part of the job, just something I happened to be doing at the time). Most importantly I got to do loads of theatre stuff – lighting designer, dresser, costumes and props, and a bit of acting too.

Later when Paul and I had parted company, I worked at the King's Head all the hours I wasn't at Drama School (every night and all day every weekend). I started in the theatre learning lighting with Dan as mentor. I was not particularly good at lights – the whole electrics thing terrified me. One night Lester, who was half-blind (and blind drunk most of the time), and myself, at that time at least three (if not four) sheets to the wind, got plucked out the bar to put back up the lights. Dan took more than half the lights down at safety inspections, and no-one ever asked if all the lights stayed the same for each performance, or if this was all of them. They just checked what was there, so no-one told any fibs – at least that's what Dan told me.

On this drunken occasion, we were standing on wobbly stools, tables and ladders, trying to do complicated electrical work. Fortunately for us, the only light that blew was one that Dan had wired.

In the early days I did quite a lot of work for nothing (or at least just for food and board), to support the theatre when the business was going through hard times (Dan showed me his books and I had access to the secret bank account). It was so bad at one time, we had to close the theatre and put a big sign out saying "Drink Cider!" as that's all we had left. This was the time just after Julian (who did time for fraud and embezzlement, while Dan kept his job open for him), and just before the manager from Belfast who famously passed a breathalyser after ten pints of Guinness (never mind driving the King's Head van, which had no MOT or probably insurance and bits dropping off it). He was on his way to 'Mick the Greek's'. I won't explain the finer points of Mick's wholesale beer business or of Dan's somewhat creative accountancy, but there was a book behind the bar which had entries in it like – 'so-and-so (borrowed) dope money', or 'staff drink some Scully or other'.

This was also after Tony (chef at the time) walked up to the bar and asked for "Half a pint of cloudy ullage in a dirty pint glass!"

He was barred for a week for telling the truth, and only allowed to walk through the bar to the kitchen.

John Scully was a local builder, who started building sets for Dan, and ended up a very talented set designer. His sets never fell down but they were a bugger to strike, they were so solidly built. His staff comprised of a vast number of young people, most of whom were his offspring, and all of whom were related. About his time I did a deal with Dan to start proper food – the chef Neil had left and the customers wanted a bit more than he was asked to provide. The kitchen was a shithole and the set menu for the theatre (smoked mackerel with bread (no garnish), charcoal grilled steak, coleslaw and a baked potato and syllabub) left much to be desired. There were regular playgoers who would eat somewhere else the second time.

I put flowers and table cloths in the bar and put on a proper menu and spent two weeks clearing up the kitchen to a catering standard. When I set it up I got my mate Jackie, who I knew from the Hackney Empire (we were doing stand-up on a sort of open mic basis there at the time) to do the days I couldn't manage, and her chef skills made this work out well. I got on quite well with the critics, and seeing the improvements, they sent their friends the food critics. My inexperience meant we had some complaints at first but eventually Jackie and I got the King's Head into the 'Egon Ronay Guide'.

On Saturdays, particularly, the band would be still playing at twelve o'clock (depending on how many bottles of whiskey we'd slipped the Old Bill at Christmas – it was 11pm closing for pubs back then). After time for a couple of songs there would be two or three women dancing naked on the bar, usually me and two others (one of the others being the manager). While this mayhem was occurring, the phone often rang – I picked it up, assuming it was someone's missus, but couldn't understand the angry screams on the other end.

"I'm sorry, I can't hear you!" I said. "There's a loud band on!"

There was a louder burst of unintelligible shrieking. I repeated "Can't hear you darlin', you'll have to speak up, there's a loud band on!"

They yelled louder. "Can you ring in about half an hour please? I still can't hear you darlin'!"

The music stopped and an even louder voice yelled "I'm ringing to complain about the noise!"

One lunchtime in the bar, I was lying across the laps of three of my lovers (sober), having a laugh (one had his hand down my pants, one was playing with my tits and the other was kissing me) – but it was all a wind-up, because I had told them one of my drama school teachers had just walked in, who also knew my Dad. The teacher glanced at me in what appeared to be a disapproving way. This irritated me a tad. I had long since decided that I was my own person, and anyway no-one else in the pub was offended, and after all actors are supposed to be given to exhibitionism aren't they? I found out later the disapproving look was a reaction to someone else's comment (a sycophant of the Principal's), and actually it was of him who disapproved. They turned out to be my greatest ally and I worked with him later at a fringe theatre.

Dan's ex-missus was still around in the early days. She still had some sort of investment in the place. I liked her. She used to tell me about the early struggle and stories about the legend that was Joe Orton. She was in cahoots with Dan's mad drunken manager. He was shagging everyone, including me (there was a bit of a 'to do' when some butter went missing from the kitchen when we were playing anal sex games).

Anyway he came to me and said, "Her Nibs and I are going to take over the pub from Dan and we'd like you to work for us."

I said, "If you do I'll work for you. If you don't I'll work for Dan, but don't underestimate Dan. I won't tell him, but he will work it out for himself if he hasn't already."

Of course Dan had, and he won. All Dan said to me was, "Did you tell them about the bank account?"

I just laughed and said, "Don't be daft!"

Anyway this manager came in legless one night and tried to throw everyone out at ten o'clock, calling time, ringing bells etc. while the staff kept telling him to fuck off upstairs and generally threw insults in his direction. Anyway there were these three idiots who decided to pick a fight with him. The manager was a long streak of piss and ten stone wringing wet (he was capable of a row but only when sober), so muggins went out to rescue him. No-one from behind the bar rushed to my support and as I was bouncer I went out to rescue the daft article! Well, two of these geezers had him pinned up against the wall and were kicking him. I pulled him out from where he was being held against the wall by getting hold of one of their arms so he could get away and screamed "Don't argue – go and get Dan, RUN!"

So he ran back into the pub and shut the door, locking the customers in, and me out with three large and livid geezers. I remember telling myself that sometimes I was a little too brave for my own good. However, having kissed more of the Blarney Stone than the drunken twit who'd got me into this shit, I mostly talked my way out of it with a minimum of fisticuffs and they went home.

During this difficult era one of the 'Money Men' turned up in a forgettable suit and with a briefcase on a Sunday morning. The three regulars were present – Gordon the Undertaker, who would tell the fireplace all the things he was pretending not to think about mourners while putting on his funeral persona. Then there was another regular drunk who sat crying at the bar. Then there was Margaret Malone's loyal 'treasure' (she was guv'nor from the next pub along Upper Street), who was noisily and defiantly telling the wall all the things he had never had the bollocks to tell Margaret in the forty odd years he'd been her live-in barman. While this cabaret was going on, Dan, in a bid to save money, in the clothes he had worn all night, was scrabbling around in the bottom of the bar end of the dumbwaiter, and was rescuing errant cutlery, chucking the filthy, greasy mess into a washing up bowl on the bar floor.

Mr 'Dreary-Suit' sauntered up to the bar, looking at me as if I'm shit off his shoe, and demanded to speak to the manager. I walked over to Dan while politely introducing him. Dan promptly climbed out the filthy lift-shaft, wiped his hand down his grubby jeans, and held it out to shake hands. The man looked horrified, but shook his hand weakly and almost ran back out of the 'madhouse' muttering something about returning at a more convenient time, never to be seen again!

The pub embraced many characters – two that come to mind were the ginger twins, so pickled with the drink I'm sure they were the source of the well-known Irish joke that goes something like this – 'Two n'er-do-wells walk in one door of a pub, get thrown out and come in the next door along (also the King's Head) and get slung out again, whilst protesting "How many fucking pubs do you run in this street?"'

Not only did I throw them out of both doors, but I had helped Margaret Malone throw them out of her pub not ten minutes beforehand (I had gone to borrow some of her beer)!

Margaret Malone, along with the rest of her Irish family, had been a 'hands on' building worker back in the old country. When she held her yearly competition to lift a firkin of Guinness above your head, 'herself' usually won, hands down!

Once there was a bit of kerfuffle at the back of the stage while a band Margaret had something to do with were setting up at the King's Head. When the sound check finished and they went for a break, Mike Khan was found out cold behind them – they'd had a bit of a bull and cow and it was rumoured Margaret was responsible. He may have been a prize fighter but she had a worse temper.

I later became a sort of resident acting ASM when I wasn't away doing something else. I was still working in the bar, and waitressing in the theatre before the show, selling tickets and so on. We worked all night and all day for about three or four nights, during the fit ups and strikes. Then I would sleep for a day before the dress rehearsal. Other people working through the night used to fill themselves full of sulphate, but generally they collapsed after the second night). I started off with 'Kennedy's Children', the first play that went straight to the West End from fringe. I watched them audition Deborah Norton for Robert Patrick. The author said to the very English lady, "Do you know what I mean by a Bronx accent, can you do something like that?" (I think it was Bronx). He told me her accent was so perfect he couldn't tell she was English. And this was the lady who told me she was not sure if she wanted to continue acting! She was later replaced by the splendid Miriam Margolyes who was a sweet lady, but one 'tough old butch thing'. as she once described herself to me.

Later I worked on Steven Berkoff's 'East'. I went out with his co-star for a while, Barry Phillips, who was fun company (in and out of bed). I think Berkoff was a bit miffed that I didn't throw myself at him like the other women did. He threw a bit of a hissy fit when he first arrived, as someone spelt his name wrong on the posters. The manager, Big Gerry, told him we didn't have stars here and wouldn't put up with all that bollocks. After that he was good as gold. I may not have fancied him but I did find him very interesting to talk to. He is an incredibly talented man with an amazingly creative mind. I have great respect for his political stance and not letting fame make him forget his roots.

I also worked on 'Spokesong' (I got to be a dab hand with a bike spanner) and got on very well with Annabel Leventon, who starred, and I ended up being listed as her understudy by Dan, after a nerve-wracking audition. I was always chatting up Stewart Parker (Spokesong's writer), and one night came in legless and fell into the bed he was sleeping in (I had forgotten Dan had given him my room). In the morning he said in his broad Belfast brogue "That's not the way to make friends, kid!" – I thought that was pretty fair, considering.

When Janis was Dan's manager, she and I were good mates, and I'm sorry I lost touch with her. Anyway, some villain she was knocking about with had given her a lighter, and while we were watching her telly she purposely used it to light the spliff I had stuck in my gob. At that very moment the lighter came up on 'Police Five' (I'm not suggesting it was nicked or anything).

Anyway she had a little place in Cornwall and we both went for a few days to have a rest (I think Dan needed the rest from both of us – particularly Janis – they were always eating each other behind the bar). When we got back there was an outbreak of customers drinking orange juice at the pub. There was a family tree type notice up in the bar, under the heading 'King's Head Clap Chart', purporting to explain who had got it from whom. For instance Potshop John's (who made ceramic toys) source of infection was his dolls. Dan's was apparently a result of shagging too many theatrical luvvies! Dan, Janis and I all went to the clinic, being the most accused and amazingly, all of us were clear! The Orphan was at the top of the chart. The Orphan was a completely feral cat. He wandered in one day, Dan and I foolishly kept feeding him so he decided to stay. Soon after he arrived he lost an eye in a fight – he was a terrible state, almost as bad as some of the customers. He had an ongoing feud with Will, who did the cellar. Being the cellar of an ancient pub (mentioned in Pepys' diary), there were places a human just couldn't get to down there, so The Orphan used to shit there just to get at Will.

I used to have a drink with Nigel Stock, who was playing the teacher in 'The Browning Version'. He was a nice man and a good drinking pal, but I made it clear I didn't fancy him, just in case that was what he had in mind. I was however interested in the actor playing the schoolboy – Richard Gibson (of 'Allo! Allo!' fame). At first I was cautious in seducing him, fooled by his aloof, upper class public school persona, but he turned out to be red hot. We were alone backstage and I could feel my nipples and his dick getting hard. While we were kissing I had him pinned up against the back wall of the small dressing room. I was writhing hard against him, causing his cock to burst out of his tight jeans and that uncontrollable heat between my legs took over, resulting in some very horny frantic sex, standing up among the costumes. At one point

I was straddled on a high dressing table, causing some poor actor's make-up being strewn all over the floor (I noticed it on the floor and put it back later before the show).

We knocked about together for a while and when we had satisfied some brief passion or other he went off with some posh bird apparently (or he was already seeing one). Besides, the play had come to the end of its run!

Anyway, Nigel also did a two hander at lunchtime with Prunella Gee called 'Carole's Christmas'. I had been teaching her to do a cockney accent, while we had a drink together. Hers was a bit Dick Van Dyke to say the least. Nigel picked up on this and suddenly decided to audition me as understudy. When I had drunk a bottle of tequila, not my fault, he and Dan conspired, and fetched me out of the bar on my night off. I ended up doing one performance while she was away doing something else.

Later we did a lesser known Tennessee Williams play called 'A Period of Adjustment', starring Tony Doyle (who was later in 'Ballykissangel' with my lovely mate Gary Wheelan), and Holly Palance (Jack's daughter), with whom I had a small but sweet scene in the play. Tony Doyle and I were drinking pals – he liked my sense of humour. I was living upstairs at this time and he said "It must be noisy upstairs with all the traffic!" and I quipped that there wasn't much traffic through my bedroom lately.

When Tennessee came to London to see the play, Mike Khan and I took him around Islington. Mike was driving us (this was not a good idea – there was no blood in his alcohol stream at the best of times). He'd bought some old sports car (and I doubt Mike had a licence), but I suppose Americans are used to cars that cough and fart and have to be pushed occasionally, seeing as most states still have no MOT. Tennessee loved Islington, the King's Head and our humble version of his play. I asked him if my performance was OK, and he said "You were very good, my dear!" – praise indeed.

I asked him why he felt he was able to write such strong parts for women. He replied "Because I am a raving queen my dear!"

Jack (Palance) came to see the play. He sat on an old grubby bench by the door (the only seat left) and told us wonderful stories about Hollywood and when he went to meet the Pope. As he was holding forth, some overzealously man-hating reporter from a feminist magazine kept asking aggressive and accusing questions, so Dan instructed me to kick her out (it was past closing and she had well overstayed her welcome big time). I was also bouncer by this time, having learned a bit of boxing and self-defence from Mike Khan. There was a bit of kerfuffle while I physically had to out her from the building (she was much bigger than me, but not as tough as she thought).

Mike had been a prize fighter in Nottingham (bare knuckles) and he and his brother were bouncers in this brothel (he told me a bizarre story about some Chinese geezer who liked to shit in a bit of newspaper). You could write a whole book about brothel stories. I've met a lot of 'ladies of leisure' in my lifetime, and each one has had a punter with a weird fetish you've never heard of before.

Anyway, me being a bit naïve and vulnerable in quite a tough part of London, he decided to teach me to look after myself. This has probably saved my life more than once, and his. He also pointed out that you had to actually put what you learned into practice and survival in an urban jungle had fuck all to do with the Marquis of Queensbury!

Mike was a hard man and he knew some naughty gangsters (I went out with one of them for a while), but he had an amazing charm and charisma, and one of the best singing voices I've ever heard. This meant he could get away with all sorts. One evening when we were all stocious, many hours after closing, Dan returned early and Mike came downstairs with a big plate of food he'd stolen from the kitchen. Wide eyed and with his impeccable comic timing he said, "I found it on the stairs – the cat wouldn't have it!"

Dan said, "Aw go on then!"

Apart from when Mike starred in a brilliant play about a rock star (we all went to see it – one of the characters said to him, "You are not in a pub full of drunks now!" and a riot nearly broke out among us pub drunks), the smoothest performance I saw of Mike's was during his version of 'Secret Love'. He would jump on the table nearest the stage in the middle of it! This one time he sang "Now I shout it from the highest hills!" – just as the table collapsed in a heap, with sound of breaking glass and furniture. Mike landed on top of it, on his feet, and sang "I even told the golden daffodils!"

He never missed a beat! He got a well deserved round of applause. With one exception I had never seen him anything but a consummate professional. The one occasion to the contrary was when Mike was going through a really bad time, and hit the drink big time. He was so pissed he could not remember the words to his own songs. When he forgot the words I yelled the next line from behind the bar. After that Dan persuaded him to take some time off!

Meanwhile, I was working on various lunchtime shows (one involved shifting a double bed up and down the stairs every day). The best was Quentin Crisp's lunchtime show 'A Cure for Freedom'. Whoever said he hated women was a homophobic wanker. He and I got on very well and he told me a lot of his wonderful stories, before I even read the play.

This is one he told me in the bar, or as much as I can remember – we were both three sheets. It goes roughly like this –

'A posh lady who has fallen on hard times, and sleeps in the park, she finds a nice dress in a bin and can't wait to try it on. As she is undressing a crowd collects, and with the crowd a policeman. When the policeman asks what she is doing she replies, "What any lady would be doing at this time of night – dressing for dinner!"'

He tells it better than I of course. At around the same time my Dad was designing the set for 'The Naked Civil Servant' on telly. So my Dad also knew him quite well. I once met Lionel Blair in the bar at the King's Head, and told him briefly that he had once worked with my Dad, Patrick Downing. I knew straight away when he said he knew Pat Downing very well, he wasn't just being polite (Dad's friends all called him Pat).

Much later on (I was with Marc by this time), Dan had employed a bloke called Sid Golder to breathe a bit of cockney working class into what had become a bit of a middle class theatre (after all it was why Dan had come from New England in the first place). Sid (an ex-bank robber turned actor) and I were old mates. We had done a Brecht play together at his Elephant Theatre (part of the South Bank Poly). Sid had rushed into the dressing room screaming "'Ere, there's some famous Hollywood geezer out there... err Tom Conteh I fink, oh I don't bleedin' know! 'Ere, come an' 'ave a look Sabena!"

Half dressed, my braces on my two-tones dragging on the floor only half grease painted, I ran out of the dressing room and ran smack bang into Dustin Hoffman, literally! I apologised profusely and he asked politely if he could come and wish the cast good luck – he did!

When Sid came backstage afterwards he was beside himself. Apparently Dustin had told Sid he had really enjoyed the play.

Anyway despite his humble beginnings, Sid was an incredibly talented and clever director and producer, and I was never sure his mistakes were not on purpose – there was a lot of the 'Columbo' about our Sid.

I had had long periods of homelessness. I did not want to sleep with someone just because I had nowhere to go like some of the people I knew (boys and girls). The street is a very dangerous place and living from hand to mouth all the time (even though I always found work) makes you feel so helpless and insecure. It cuts into your self-esteem, especially if you are not very confident in the first place.

I ended up sleeping rough. I tried Finsbury Park but you were too isolated to be safe. If you could avoid being moved on by coppers, the streets were much safer – eventually I ended up behind the lockers in King's Cross station. There was a gap where you couldn't be seen between the lockers and the wall.

People on the street are like a family with no room for snobbery or prejudice. As far as the rest of the world is concerned, you are all the same scum, yet the prostitutes, junkies and drunks – if it was not for them I would not have survived! I don't follow any religion, but it is to them and the Salvation Army that I owe my life.

CHAPTER FIVE
Islington, Among Other Places

Lester was Dan's (the manager's) latest general dogsbody. I was mostly to pay for his huge intake of lager. His best mate, Duncan, was a costumier. When he had an opportunity for someone who could do some sewing and a bit of acting he took me. So I was off again, out to very Welsh Wales (Narberth mainly), where we made 'The Mouse and the Woman'.

Most of it was costume and extra work, but I had a small speaking part as a maid. We stayed at the Welsh Kitchen, a bed and breakfast that has never been the same since. Unfortunately Duncan employed a friend to help – Ilian. Ilian and Duncan fell out and Duncan went home. By this time Duncan was drinking rum from seven in the morning, and the stress of an impossible amount of cossies on a low budget had taken its toll on him. Duncan was a splendid fella and contributed to my reputation as a 'fag hag' (an offensive phrase used as an insult by homophobes in less enlightened times, but I wore the insult like a badge).

I liked Ilian (who was a fashion designer, not a costumier), and we got on OK, but Duncan was correct about one thing – his concept of what they wore in Wales during the First World War was vague. I suppose he did his best with what we had. The film was a success for Karl Francis (replete with standing ovation at Cannes) and although I had my altercations with him (I didn't want to shag him just to be in the film, and he took exception to the fact that I was shagging everybody else), I met some brilliant people while I was there and have a lifelong love of Wales, as I do Ireland.

As well as doing a job I wanted to do, it generated a lot of sexual relationships, some of which I can't talk about for various reasons. However I had a lot of exciting and memorable one night stands, which I didn't pretend were going to end up in matrimony, although through all the fun and naughtiness, I have to admit I was very fond of Henry. When nobody could find me on a morning where they needed to start early (there was the right amount of snow on a mountain) they looked in several people's beds before they discovered me calmly eating breakfast in the Welsh Kitchen, wondering what all the fuss was about. I had been at Henry's house.

The best bit of the film, in my humble opinion, was the firing squad at the mill. It was also pretty scary when the blanks were being fired in our direction and we had to duck (there was nowhere else for us to go without being in shot). Even though my one line did not even get me a cast listing, I still think this was a brilliant film, so much better than a lot of the drivel from the US we are all being subjected to now.

While I was touring with Bristol Gate, I had moved to Redland in Bristol, into an attic flat with a nice middle class family who had a really handsome seventeen year old (who was a virgin, at least up until we met). It was fun at first, and the frantic fumbling whilst trying not to be discovered by his parents was very horny, but after a while he I think the novelty of experienced older woman thing wore off (I was only about twenty). I decided to behave as his nice parents were becoming quite protective and kept saying things like 'you smell like Sabena' when we came out of his room (I used to wear patchouli oil).

I had become weary with travelling to where the others lived in St. Paul's (where the riots were later in the eighties). I liked all the reggae clubs, and blues parties, but it was a pain to get back to posh Redland, so I started going to pubs in Clifton. I went out with one docker and ended up living with his mate for a while in Clifton. I later went for an interview on the Avonmouth Docks myself with the excuse that I was engaged to a docker (I wasn't really but it was a closed shop). It was before the Sex Discrimination Act but the gaffer decided to humour me and booked me for a day's trial. I was very fit at the time, and had been doing so called 'men's' jobs for quite a while, so as an ardent feminist I felt I had to take up the challenge (although I had no intention of becoming a docker).

Anyway, although it was freezing in the container with just a donkey jacket, I was able to compete physically and was put on the list. That evening I went to the docker's club. Women were not allowed in the docker's club, nor had one ever ordered a pint in there before, but the local gaffer looked on his clipboard, saw my name and said, "She's a docker my lover, you'd better give her a pint!"

This was my third encounter with 'men's jobs' – my second was on a building site, when I desperately needed to find the deposit for a flat to escape from some 'orrible squat, back when I had split up with Paul. A mate (known as Darlow) from a pub I used to work in (the Old King's Head, when I worked for Keith and Lesley in Holloway Road) had just come over from Belfast to work on the demolition. He had seen me manhandling some drunk after time and knew I did weights at the Sobel. He told me where the site was and the name of the gaffer. I walked up to him and said I understood he had a job for a strong labourer (he asked if it was for my boyfriend).

I said I was stronger than my boyfriend, and mainly to have a laugh, he stood down a hole and told one of the lads to give me a fifteen pound hammer, and to knock this bit of brick sticking up out of the hole. Not being used to the power of the hammer or my own strength I knocked it off and most of the side of the hole collapsed. He got out coughing and spluttering from the flying plaster and said "I can see you are strong enough for the job, but we will have to tame you."

He took me to another site, where they had knocked down a small building and asked me to make good. Clear up all the mess and scaffolding boards. In about three hours I had finished, but as I went back to the site they had moved on to the next one. Darlow predicted this so he gave me the address of the new one (quite close by). When I arrived he was stunned and started to believe I really wanted a job and might be useful. He took me back to the old site to look at my work and asked who helped me. There were some lads building on the other side of the site and they confirmed I'd done all the lifting myself so he gave me a job in the East End. When I got to the site it was an old fashioned block of flats and instead of burning rubbish with the younger lads he sent me up on the roof. No hard hat, no harness, no health and safety, no walls – just stairs to the roof, held up by wobbly scaffolding. I was petrified but dare not show it! I worked with a nice older man who neither tried to chat me up nor patronise me. He taught me how to balance on a sloping roof to remove the slate (and probably saved me from a serious accident, for which I am very grateful). We looked like miners when we finished – the roof was covered in soot from the old fashioned chimneys.

I did quite a lot of bits of theatre during this period. We toured an anti-nukes play called 'Come Fry With Me'! It was an amalgamation of Unity and The Hampstead Theatre Club – who were not as posh as they sound. I had seen a lot of work there, in particular two anti-racist plays, a lot earlier, for which my Dad designed the sets. I have absolutely no dancing skills and two left feet, so I was very proud that I did so well in this musical, particularly a complicated dance for one number in six inch heels, whilst singing, smiling and looking as though I was confident (although I was terrified). This was achieved by rehearsing every hour of the day until I got it right – we got splendid notices.

Before that I was in a musical called 'Pucka Ri'. This was set after a nuclear explosion, but it was actually a very upbeat musical that did well at the Edinburgh Festival. Of course, the fact that we were all naked apart from the all-over green body paint didn't hurt the box office.

While working with the Bristol Gate theatre company, we performed in the grounds of Salisbury Cathedral. People who know me may find this hard to believe, but me and the Archbishop of Canterbury Robert Runcie, who was overseeing the proceedings with the Bishop of Salisbury, got on extremely well. I used to get told off for calling him Bish, but I was instrumental in persuading him not to charge to go into the Cathedral.

Anyway, there was a local fair going on in the grounds and I pulled one of the fairground workers (gorgeous big hunky thing – I got used to the Brummie accent). I had stayed a couple of nights in his caravan. I gave him my phone number and promised to catch up with them when we did a gig in their hometown Smethwick, where we happened to be gigging later. So after the company had finished all its gigs I went back to Islington, after a few months in Smethwick, living on a proper Romany encampment, and off the radar for a bit. After a while, his rather more traditional Dad gave me the impression that it was the done thing to get married, but I had made no such promises, so after about four months I decided it was time to go back to Islington. I did learn a bit about Birmingham and bit about travellers and had a great deal of fun (I told you when I came I was a stranger). One of my mates at the time pointed out that I had itchy feet and even the travellers couldn't pin me down!

After moving from Smethwick I did some more acting, staying on a commune in Swindon and touring theatre in education inside and around inflatable balloons with 'Ground-Well Farmers' (an offshoot of the Bubble Theatre). Aside from actors there were potters, basket weavers and a full time vegetable grower and goatherd – all of which this city girl ended up being quite good at, I might add among others – and nobody signed on! But I met a lovely lady called Caroline (who ended up staying with me later).

As we were finishing up in Bristol, I went back to the King's Head to work on 'Smith and Goody' (Mel Smith and Bob Goody). They were a great laugh. I used to have a drink with Mel, who used to talk a lot about horses and gambling (I had already learned quite a bit from Charlie – mainly that the only winner is the bookie). Spookily, the day after we struck the set I bumped into him in the middle of Bristol at a bus stop. We went for a coffee (it was freezing) where we discussed politics until he had to be at some meeting about his next project.

I also tried my hand at the Comedy Store briefly where I met Dawn French (she was the nicest of them, with the warmest personality). Alexei Sayle was compère there at the time, and later I ended up doing some admin work for his 'Threepenny Theatre' group. I tried to book gigs for him but was pretty naff at it. I really hoped to do some acting but it really happened before the group folded and we all went our separate ways, so I moved on.

I did a great gig for 'Time Out' at the Lyceum Ballroom. At the time I had only been on small stages in fringe theatres and the like (even in Madrid). The stage at the Lyceum is like an aircraft hangar, although the compère was Jeremy Beadle, who was lovely and very professional. I was still terrified, which wasn't helped by my guitarist (Tony Crosby – more about him later). He was too pissed to stand up, so as I was dressed as a Victorian policeman (don't ask) I arrested him and removed him from the stage whilst whispering gently in his ear, "Fuck off or I'll knock you out again, you're off your crust!"

I thought it was going to be a complete disaster. I suddenly realised as I was singing 'Shine On Harvest Moon' that the audience had stopped yelling "Fuck off, we want Hank Wangford!" and were swinging their elbows from side to side and singing along. I thought, "Fuck me, I've got 'em!"

Any performer that says they don't love that feeling of power that performers get when they have got the audience's attention is a liar.

In the early days Mike's gigs were just him and Malcolm mainly, with the band at the weekends – whichever talented musicians were knocking about at the time. In the very early days I did some backing singing in the studio. It was about the time that a lovely lady called Mary Rainbow went off to do something else as well. Mike and I had been lovers previously from time to time, but later on when our relationship became more brother and sisterly, and I was off doing my acting, he found other backing singers. Mike liked to work with women he was screwing as much as I liked to screw the musicians in his band. Hanging around at Mike's was great for my cultivated groupie image (not to mention my libido). There were lots of occasions when I indulged in gang bangs with three or more men (and on rare occasions women, although that was mostly because I enjoyed the voyeuristic sexual pleasure men got from women playing with each other rather than any personal bisexual preference).

We were all adults in a close-knit circle of friends. Mike had nicknamed me Kemo Sabe (as in the Lone Ranger, a theory at the time being that Charles Larson meant it as a joke, the translation being 'White Trash' in Comanche and I was the only white one of the cohorts). I also often got called Sabby. Our lovely mate George Khan (no relation to Mike) was around a lot at this time. He was working with the People Show among other things (with Mark Long, Emil Wolk and Chahine Yavroyan). George still did guest appearances playing sax in Mike's band when he was available. He had his own band called 'Mirage'. I remember them well, not only because they were brilliant (funky music) but because when they descended upon the King's Head, Dan had somewhat underestimated their popularity, so there was just he and I working the bar. It was that night, particularly, despite my dyscalculia I learned to add up five rounds at once in my head. Dan and I took the King's Head's first grand (just bar takings). Later in his very successful acting career he got a part in 'The Fifth Element'. George told me he was lucky, because his family taught him how to 'show off' and he said his ability to get noticed got him work (he didn't mention his extraordinary talent and obsessive hard work). He told me about his mime training with Marcel Marceau and how intensive and hard mime was.

I have not seen George for a long time but I know he is still working with the People Show, as well as his other work, so I know he has not lost his roots. He was probably the most together of all of us, although he did fracture Mike's wrist one night to stop him belting some idiot who was winding him up (he knew Mike would have gone to prison as he was on a suspended sentence). George was very good to me in the early days, he was a sort of mentor and elder statesman who gave me some good advice that stayed with me.

One night when we were all round Mike's, a certain someone (who will be nameless) was getting married the next day, so he was shagging this woman round at Mike's, with everyone sitting round watching (yeah, I know – I asked him why the hell he was getting married too). She seemed to be interested in involving Mike and well up for it, then she changed her mind when the other bloke (who was getting married the next day) started being possessive or protective (I'm not sure which). A fight ensued nevertheless and you can see clearly in the photos, both the groom and the best man (Mike) had purple shiners. God knows what he said to his bride!

I was spending a lot of time at Mike's, he used to like the fact that I cleaned up his place for him. It was about this time our mate Roy Minton had written a brilliant TV series called 'Scum' and Mike sung the theme tune 'Wide Boy' (you can still find it on the web). For whatever reason (probably the rape scene) the telly series never happened and they made the film instead. Well, anyway, Roy was quite pissed one night and staying round Mike's. He had come straight down from Nottingham and was knackered so he nodded off on Mike's sofa. There were about eight of us (apart from Roy) indulging in some sort of drunken sex, mostly writhing around on the floor with multiple partners in some sort of orgy. Every time Roy woke up Mike and I had different partners. Roy registered what was going on, threw his eyes up in the air, then went back to sleep – this happened three or four times (to my knowledge). I should explain Mike and I had a platonic sort of thing going by this time, less like siblings, and more like partners in crime. I was his confidant and he mine. Mike was still booking music at the Kings Head, including bands like Café Racers (Mark Knofler's band that turned into Dire Straits) and Café Society, Tom Robinson's band. Bad Manners also played there (they were a blues band then). I still have a picture of Buster Bloodvessel with long hair (more about him later), although I did not know him at the time. Brilliant acts like Diz Watson, Ronnie Kavanagh and the Balham Alligators with Robin McKidd were also regular acts in the bar. Later came Red Beans & Rice and the gorgeous Laverne Brown (he told me how a load of 'redskins' had to rescue him from Madness's accidental racist following – when he was supporting them at one gig, he thought he was going to be lynched). Later Madness decided to take a more political stance, and the idiots seemed to bugger off and leave them alone.

My last move had been when I left Bristol. In order to move all my gear, I had asked a very kind mate who was the only person I knew with transport to help me cart what was left of my possessions (that hadn't been thieved in some squat) back to the King's Head loft. His car was a Bentley (you have to be a millionaire to drive in London anyway, and he happened to be a millionaire). I had offered to pay the petrol, but he said, "I'm not being funny darlin', but you couldn't afford petrol for this."

He and his Missus (who designed glasses for Rayburn) were kind hearted people and he took me anyway. So this time, not wanting to take advantage, I decided to take my stuff to my new flat on the 73 bus. After all, when I was cheffing in the Kings Head (when I wasn't shifting pianos, barrels, or huge basketball players), I had been known to bring half a side of beef back from Smithfield on the 73. Also I once bought a whole goat back on the bus, I had to retrieve it from the bar staff, who had propped it up on a stool at the bar and were trying to feed it drinks. They were a mad bunch of bastards.

I was fed up with having no money because London Fringe is always an on/off thing. So I got myself a better paid job as a youth worker at Clapton Youth Centre. I had been in a theatre group with this very political bloke, whose wife was a teacher. They had cajoled the Council into this project, running an educational Youth Centre at an old boys club in Canning Town. He was pretty tough and from some warzone in Africa, but she was finding it difficult to cope with the sweet young things of Canning Town, so he asked me if I would come and help. By her own admission she was a posh girl from York and the kids had been left to their own devices and were running wild. I started by confiscating all weapons and instilling some ground rules, but it was an uphill struggle. Having been a former boys club, the young people were divided into boys and girls. Boys played football so they had given the girls a room of their own, out of the way. I started off with in the girls' room getting them to sing pop songs, we then tried choreographing some dance moves to go with them. It was hard to the boys involved in anything that was not criminal at first. Then I taught them other songs from musicals, when we started rehearsing a show. Seeing the girls involved in something new excited the boy's curiosity. The show was quite successful, and even some reluctant parents turned up and participated in the group.

So when I got taken on at Clapton I already had some experience and had taught some drama. Clapton was far ahead of most youth clubs. It was run by Anslem Samuel – Sam (Head Tutor) and Jean Tate (Tutor Manager). It had a written anti-racist policy and was considered a safe haven for young people against a white racist society. Although the majority of young people there were black, this reflected the local community and a lot of white young people attended, because they respected what the Centre was trying to achieve. This brave (for the time) anti-racist political assertion was considered dangerous by the right wing government of the day and the sabotage was blatant, and led right up to the top levels of the Party, and the crooked opposition included top police chiefs and many political bigwigs. When eventually Clapton closed, they used some underhanded excuse and I was sent to work at other youth centres. I started off at Holloway, the politics of which were so entwined with the right wing perpetrators of the girl's school behind it that no-one dare breathe, let alone do something radical or intelligent to better the lives of the young people who used it. Following that was Hoxton, which was a centre for criminal chaos the like of which I've only ever encountered elsewhere whilst visiting prisons. Just getting there was a nightmare. The only possible route to work was through a myriad of drug gang infested estates, whose sentries would demand to know my reason for being there. Once I had explained, I moved through the next border control (Hoxton's staff were considered the good guys, as most of them seemed to be entwined with the local mafia they were unlikely to grass).

The married youth worker I was assigned to work with was sleeping with many of the young people she was supposed to be supporting with absolutely no regard for the age of consent. Her racist attitude was that black young men were fair game. Heroin use was rife. I went to throw some very large young men out of an unattended upstairs snooker room, where they were chasing the dragon. One of them threw me on the table and another jumped on top of me and started a sort of pretend fucking, then another lad tried to join in. I was not waiting to find out if the physical and verbal threat of gang rape was the joke their laughter may have signified. I threw him off me and fetched him a volley of punches, causing him later to sport a black eye and bruised chin, screaming, "Right you bastards, who's next?"

Apart from the bravado I was hoping to get the attention of one of the idiots I worked with. They never grassed me up, nor I them, but I had no more trouble with any of the big lads. It was a tacit agreement of mutual respect. The nicer faction of Hackney's teenagers, who normally spent time at Clapton, were forced to hang about in snooker halls and amusement arcades, where crime was rife. The crime rate doubled and gave us an unforeseen ally. Eventually Clapton's white racist police demanded it be reopened, but the political backlash meant a 'reorganisation of staff'.

Dan had run out of managers and the one he wanted to run the place was doing time for fraud and embezzlement. Of course this did not put any kind of question on his honesty working for Dan, or his ability to run the pub (and indeed when he took over he was a splendid manager), but there was no one he could trust while he went off and sorted out some of the mess left by his ex and the Irish manager, except little old me. It was a lot of responsibility for me to run the pub for two weeks. I was still very young and naïve, and God awful at maths.

I should explain – one of Dan's foibles, and part of his American bloke who loves everything English obsession, meant everything was in pre-decimal currency. The staff charged in old money, although they took decimal currency, added up in old money and all the books (even VAT) was in pounds, shillings and pence. My one saving grace was that the people who worked there at the time were like a family. Amazingly, apart from one awful moment when I thought the dosh was seriously short, before I remembered notes got stuck down the back of the ancient till, the whole thing went off smoothly. I was very grateful as everyone knew they could have nicked loads easily.

When Dan returned, I was back living in 'Birdbrain's Perch' so to get rid of me, he said. Dan agreed to let the man from the council look at my 'temporary accommodation' amongst the props and costumes in the loft. (I was apparently Islington's first single woman who wasn't pregnant who was given a council flat – I just wore them down with polite persistence, along with a sound knowledge of my rights). Dan was very good – he said he couldn't see me out on the street and it was my only choice by then. They were fed up with me sitting in the Council office, so the council geezer (who was sympathetic) came to the King's Head, eventually, asking if I wanted to 'view' a flat in Newington Green. I was like a pig in shit – anyone who has been homeless will know once you have your own place you never look back, unless you're a twat and cock it all up for yourself.

I said to him, "I don't want to view it – I'm homeless, mate. Just give me the keys!"

He said, "But you might not like it!"

I said, "Has it got a roof?"

He said, "Yes!"

I said, "I LIKE IT! Give me the keys!"

He laughed and gave me the keys and the address and I moved in. Immediately!

CHAPTER SIX
Hope and Anchor

When I stopped working for youth centres, because of the political complications, I went back to work for Dan full time – but the constant bartering for wages was beginning to piss me off in the end. I was also fed up with Dan's various women, who would move in and, soon as they were 'on the firm', start ordering everyone about (almost without exception they were women of expensive educations, but no fucking common sense and were bollocks at running pubs). So as I wasn't living there any more I decided it was probably time to move on.

I started drinking in the Hope and Anchor. Big Mick did the door (later dubbed Mick the Gorilla by me due to his inability to straighten up in the morning – his arms would dangle in front of him before the first cup of coffee). Mick the Gorilla got me a job behind the bar and on the door, and later he moved into the flat with me. If I must give it a label, let's say it was an open relationship for about seven years, and although we are now both happy in monogamous relationships, I don't regret a moment of it. We may have both worked hard but we had loads and loads of fun!

Quite soon after Mick moved in, I did an audition as a bluecoat at Caister Holiday Camp, near Great Yarmouth. I did not know much about holiday camps, except where Nan and Charlie had taken me, so I prepared a nice audition speech. While people were auditioning I was standing by the piano being my usual sarcastic self (not about anyone's performance except mine, I hasten to add).

Then the fellow in charge said, "Right, your turn – have you got any music?"

I didn't even know I what was going to sing, but playing it by ear, I sang 'One of the Ruins that Cromwell Knocked About a Bit' and made it extra filthy. He really liked it, but said I would need something else for the main ballroom (obviously meaning it was too naughty for kids), so I sang Burlington Bertie. Not only did I pass but he thought all the ad-libbed patter was my comedy routine.

Little did he know I was going there to thieve jokes off comedians to write my own stand-up. I did tell the comedians at the camp I intended to steal their jokes and they were only too glad to help and gave me gags to use. Although I was by far the naughtiest bluecoat, there were some interesting situations that I was not even party to – like two drunk bluecoats (one girl, one boy) still in full uniform sitting (passed out) in the bath and one (boy) passed out on the bathroom floor. There were lots of drugs at the camp. The security guards were always covering for us.

My favourite comedian Phil loved to grass up the bluecoats while announcing them to the campers. For example, the head bluecoat passed out on the balcony of one venue after the campers had gone home and slept there the night. When his time to come on stage came, Phil announced this poor visibly hungover man thus – "And here we have, live from the Holiday Inn balcony…!"

I stayed chatting one night in the chalet of a guest comedian, who was married. Actually it was not like that – we *were* talking, but there was no telling Phil. "And here she is, live from the divorce courts…!"

Considering how ordinary the place was, the bluecoats were a wild bunch – no doubt I was considered the wildest, as I was so blatant about my horniness and notch on the bed attitude to sex that most people only expected of men then-a-day. It caused a big problem with one gentleman who had neglected to inform me he was engaged to a girl in the kitchen, while obviously succumbing to my advances in front of witnesses. Needless to say, by the time I got to the morning meeting, the engagement was off. I got a lot of stick, defending myself to those whose business that it wasn't, by pointing out that I don't have ESP, and if I'd known I would not have partaken of that particular delight. This didn't help either.

Later in the season I ended up falling in love, with a lovely man who probably ended up as a professional rugby player, if he managed to stop damaging himself whilst playing it. All sorts of bits of him were broken, but not the tackle though – that was in perfect working order. He was an ex public school boy and a student from a posh family, who had a degree to finish, and I doubt Mummy and Daddy would have approved. So I knew I would have to move on, as Leonard Cohen said –

"And then leaning on your windowsill
He'll say one day you caused his will
To weaken with your love and warmth and shelter
And then taking from his wallet
An old schedule of trains, he'll say
I told you when I came I was a stranger
I told you when I came I was a stranger."

I was still doing loads of auditions. I couldn't sight read well at all, but I passed one, where they gave me a book and said "Read this phrase as Northern Irish, this in Geordie, this phrase in Scouse...!" etc.. Usually I just got on with it, but this time, with an unusual surge of taking the bull by the horns, I said to them "Look! I can't just read things like that, but if you give me a moment on my own with it, I'll come back and do it."

They went for it, I did it well and they gave me the job. It was a Christmas show at the Oval – don't ask me what it was called, I can't remember, but I remember actually doing the show. It was great!

Back in Islington I worked back at the 'Hope'. I was working behind the bar with Eamonn Rodrigues – that's what he called himself then (actually his second name is Roderique), now a successful actor called Eamonn Walker. His 'Othello' on the telly was brill, and he's now in 'Chicago Fire' playing the Chief. Eamonn had just finished at the Anna Scher Theatre acting school. I was supposed to be sharing my talent for bar work, but he had other talents I wanted to share. He ended up staying with me and Mick – at least that's what we told his very religious Mum, who said "I'm glad you and your husband are looking after Eamonn – he is a bit wild!"

Actually Mick was knocking about with a woman called Ali, who hung around with Madness, and Eamonn was staying with me. I remember how young he was, as we had a birthday party for him, and John the guv'nor assumed it was his nineteenth, but actually he was only eighteen, but had been behind the bar for a year, having lied about his age.

Anyway he was doing a dance class in a church hall in Upper Street. So I attended. There were about thirty women in his dance class, and Eamonn was shagging all of us. I had been friendly with Eamonn's older brother Eric, before his tragic death (Eric's death, and the downfall of a very talented musician and singer, was triggered by some idiot spiking his drink with acid at a party – I hope this twat realised at some point what they had done). Anyway, Eamonn and I were in a play together at the Octagon, where we kept saying each other's lines. Of course, confident Eamonn had no problems with that, but terrified Sabena dried in performance and made a complete arse of herself (although Eamonn did try to get me out of trouble, I was still helpless).

Me, Eamonn and Mick were big mates in the early days. The sexual attraction fizzled out after a while (we were both playing the field), but we remained mates for a good while. I went out with lots of men who worked or played at the Hope – one of them was an area organiser for the British Movement (I did not know this when I pulled him). He worked with Eamonn and they were quite good mates, but having a mate who was black, albeit only a workmate, caused a conflict of interest, causing him to leave the BM and join a soul band (all of whom were black) – last I heard he was playing with Howlin' Wolf!

John Eichler, the governor of the Hope (Mick the Gorilla nicknamed him the 'Eichlertollah' after the Ayatollah Khomeini – this was an indication of power, rather than religion) was just organising a series of charity gigs called 'Blanket Coverage'. It included every famous band that had played there – probably every punk, ska, rockabilly etc. band you can remember if you were around at the time. Madness (then the 'North London Invaders') spent a lot of time at the pub. I knew the lads a bit. When they first came in they were still wearing school uniforms. They were talking about a rehearsal one day and I asked if they were actors – they explained they were a band but were going to rehearse for a year before doing a gig. They were nice lads – despite their working classness they were well educated with quite well to do parents, most of whom seemed to live in Primrose Hill (a posh bit of Camden). I did some roadie work for them, if you can call it that (I was strong but I did not drive and I was no expert). They used to call me Sabrina to take the piss. I was filmed in the pub for a promotional film, but I doubt I was in the finished product. I don't think Dave Robinson liked me much. Chas and Brendon his brother, together with Suggs and I had a drink or three one night, and they explained all their songs on the album. They had told me earlier (I don't know if it's true) that they marketed 'The Prince' by going into all the dance halls mob-handed and threatening the DJs with violence if they didn't play it. Whatever the truth, it rocketed into popularity!

There were lots of people knocking about the place at that time and I was talking to Annie Lennox about men and their attributes (it was about sex). Mick the Gorilla dubbed us 'Vodka and Coke' – I was vodka, although it could have been the other way round! Hanging around Annie was a roadie who worked for 'Bad Manners' I was giving a load of old chat, who turned out to be spoken for. The roadie introduced to me to Dougie (Buster Bloodvessel) and I ended up taking him back to mine.

We spent plenty of time together after that, here and there. He took me back to his mum's flat one time, near Manor House. He was supposed to be on a diet, but his Mum had left him the biggest salad you have ever seen. I said to him, "That's not really a diet, is it?"

He said she spoilt him because he'd had a hard time and he was adopted. I don't believe he was spoilt though. He was far too nice and down to earth to be spoilt – I think she just loved him. Anyway, he wanted to learn the cancan. I pointed out that although I knew the steps, I was no dancer – in fact I was a clumsy fucker. Now, it was the thing in that part of London at the time for ladies to collect lots of little ceramic ornaments (all the women in my family had them), and Dougie's mum had hundreds of the bleeding things, all very breakable. As the two less than balletic people jumped about (this was the middle of a high rise block, at one point – the neighbours shouted and banged on the floor), these things were bouncing all over the place and I could see me getting in big trouble with his mum. However I did teach him the cancan and he was much better at it than it looked at gigs, where he made it funnier. He played me three endings to the song – I think I chose one, but I thought they were all good.

One night, he got some money from Magnet and took me to this wine bar in Stoke Newington. We were both on diets (I was acting in something and doing these clothing catalogues) and were staying on the white wine – however, this poncey wine bar didn't have any house white left so we drunk copious amounts of red wine. On our way home we were singing – he started singing the verse to a song they were writing.

"I'm just a-walking in the sunshine
Leave your troubles all behind you..."

He said, "I can't think of a next line." We'd been going on about how shit this wine bar was, not having any white wine – he sang this a few times, then I sang, "I think I'll drink a little red wine!" – or something similar. Anyway, they used it in the song – I'm quite proud of that.

I didn't see Dougie often, but when I did it was always explosively sexual (although we did manage to talk sometimes). He explained that he used to do tongue exercises like actors do and then used it as part of his performance persona. As you can imagine, the real person was very adept with that tongue. It kept me amused for hours, but that is not the only part of his body he was good with. For someone who pretended to be clumsy he was a very gentle and adept lover. He would slide his tongue gently down the inside of my thighs until I was shuddering and could not stand any more. He would tease me until I physically pulled him on top of me, screaming out for penetration (it may seem ordinary, but like many other women it's the bit I like best). The hardness and his excitement meant I could not hold back for long and would I would erupt really quickly, but he was never far behind. It's difficult to admit but I was absolutely smitten (I wrote poetry and everything), but I never told him so. By this time I was acutely aware of how famous he had become and I imagined loads of women were chucking themselves all over him. Probably had women all over the shop, and especially as I was a bit older and a struggling actress, I came to realise that we were probably not going to end up in a proper relationship, so I cried a bit, remembered how good it was, and moved on.

I was still hanging around with Mike's band and Mike threatened to keep a list of how many lead guitarists I had slept with, as compared with drummers etc.! I was going out with a guitarist who was in a band called 'Sons of Fat Harry', as they played in a bar called 'Fat Harry's' after the villain that owned it (I think I'll get away with calling him this without repercussions...). They played gentle, almost folky music, which is why it amused me that Lemmy from Motorhead often busked with them. He was very interesting to talk to and thought we had met before at one of his gigs at Eel Pie Island. He had some interesting political views and, despite wearing iron crosses, was furiously anti-racist, anti-sexist and anti-Nazi!

I continued to be my normal naughty self, including sneaking on stage to sing along with UB40 and The Tourists in the early days. There was a fabulous gig with 999 (I wish I had a copy of the photo). People kept pogoing onto the stage (it was fashionable at the time), so all these huge geezers stood in front of the stage and held hands in the middle, and at the most difficult place, where it curved, was little old me! Mike around this time was sharing a studio with Roxy Music – he and Bryan Ferry (who was very up himself at the time) did not get on. Bryan and he had a slight altercation about them overrunning and Bryan tried to play the hard man. Mistake – Mike knocked him out with one punch! I don't think they shared a studio again (I got told off for laughing).

A little later I went to an iffy audition. First of all it was in 'Cat's Alley' (Wardour Street in Soho) – secondly the ad intimated some sort of nudity. I had been to a couple of iffy auditions before (one where some big fat man was going to make me a famous model if I screwed him, or some such crap), and I done some innocuous soft porn and naughty photos for a couple of mags, so I was quite *au fait* with the seedier side of trying to get an equity card, and took Mick for protection. It turned out to be a cover for some other naughtiness I best not go into, but some of which you will find out later. What they were doing was ostensibly a live sex show (at least that's what it said on the board outside) – in fact it was a short play with a bit of nudity and some very unsexy so-called actors. It wasn't going well and he wanted to replace the cast. What we ended up with was me and a bunch of much more talented people, who were mostly feeding their smack habits, not that this bothered me as long as I did not sit on any needles. One was some singer from the band 'The Regents' and also Mikey Barson's sister was there for a while. Barry, the club manager, was mates with Suggs' parents.

The original script was written by Sandy Fawkes (In Praise of Younger Men), who was going out with Barry. I expect it was short, as it was written in between drinks at the French House. I liked Sandy – drunk and abusive as she was, she never turned her venom on me and told some wonderful stories, including about nearly being murdered by a serial killer. I was so interested I ended up reading her book about it (Killing Time).

Anyway, with her permission we made it better, funnier and longer. Mick ended up as one of the bouncers. People used to pay quite a high entrance fee, saw the show and then got turfed out the back door (where all the brothels were in the mews). Many of them used to come back to the front door and tell Roger it was a total rip-off, but it was very funny and they really enjoyed it. The sex was all pretend, although quite horny to watch apparently (well, the men that watched it seemed to think so, because they were always getting caught cracking one off). We dubbed it the 'Lie Sex Show'.

One day there was only one bloke in the audience. Barry was concerned he might be a copper. We had already had one raid, in which a bloke had jumped on stage – I jumped three paces backwards, thinking it was a punter, then the bouncers jumped up as well, then he flashed a warrant card and all they did was warn Barry about not having a theatre licence.

Anyway, Nigel suggested that if he was a copper, he would jump up before the show and shout "Hello! Hello! Hello! What ISN'T going on here?!"

The aforementioned doorman, Roger the Dodger, was one of those cockneys whose entire rhetoric, which he spoke at 100 miles per hour, consisted of the first word. This is one of his that I managed to once follow – "He was in the rub, trying to blag this Richard, when she pours her ruby right over his uncle, knocks off his syrup and he falls on his Aris!"

He was in the pub, trying to chat up a bird, when she pours her curry over his head, knocks off his wig and he falls on his arse (arse is a double rhyming slang – Aristotle = bottle, bottle and glass = arse).

There was a building site next door to the club, and I fancied the pants off this builder. I gave him a lot of old chat, but his mates were always hanging about. One evening, his mates seemed to disappear, things got really heated and we started rolling around the building site shagging wildly. I did not realise his mates were watching until he sat me up on this low scaffolding so he could stand up on a bit of concrete to get better purchase. I could see his mates watching out of the corner of my eye. Whilst flailing about I threw my head up in the air and could see the entire cast from the club watching out the window, waving their arms and pointing. I was too engrossed in what I was doing to be concerned. When we had finished, eventually (he was well fit), they all gave us a round of applause. They left the next day, so I didn't get a chance for a return match.

In the evenings I enjoyed the Soho scene. I didn't have a bank account so the gov'nor kept my wages in his safe at the Swiss Tavern (My Swiss bank account). I was going to spend half of them there anyway! During the day it was full local villains, pimps and Ladies of the Night, some of whom I became good mates with for a while (two of them went on to form a professional Caribbean rock band). 'Afters' started as soon as the door was locked (I was often spending the night with one or two of the barmen upstairs) – people like Tom Baker used to put their hand flat on the window above the curtains to gain access. The Old Bill caught on and tried this – the gov'nor poked his head out the door and said to the plain clothes policeman, "Sorry officer, we close at eleven – you ought to know that!"

He must have suspected they were trying it on to bust him as it wasn't his usual Old Bill (like Upper Street, the patrons of Soho were not normally averse to a bit of bribery). Of course the pub was heaving, but they couldn't get in without a warrant, even for a late drink. Black Bob, the barman I spent most time with, was a one-eyed aging alcoholic, who shagged all the local whores. People did not understand the attraction but there was something about him that I found really sexy! He knew what women wanted and how to give it to them.

The gay glitterati of the time used to take part in the Soho pram race. This piece of local chaos and insanity consisted of lots of blokes in drag pushing other blokes dressed as babies who raced each other for charity, completely off their heads. There were some gay women dressed as dads and me pushing Bob, who was the ugliest baby you have ever seen – made a fortune for the gay switchboard! This bit of nonsense was the precursor to the Pride marches – such a wonderful day and one I will never forget!

There was also the Duke of Welly up the road – I often stayed there with an attractive young barman or two. The governor, Nick, took over a pub in Islington I'll talk about later. Bob used to take me on a Soho pub crawl in his break. I've never drunk so much beer in such a short time before or since – we did at least seven pubs in an hour. Much later when I was a civil servant, a very prissy religious colleague insisted on following me to the Bengali Centre to check up on me. I did warn her she would not like walking through Soho, but she insisted. As we walked down Wardour Street every rough looking bouncer, lady of the night scratching their track marks, rentboy just on his way home and several other nefarious characters said, "Watcha Sabena – how's Peter Everard, etc. etc.?" (a character from the show). She decided not to accompany me next time my Bengali chefs project took me that way!

If I wasn't watching a band, I would go and drink in Gerry's Club, where all the actors were. Paul Raymond was often in the company I drank with, and gave me a load of old chat one night ostensibly offering me a job in his 'Revue Bar'. I pointed out that I was no dancer, so his sudden interest was a bit obvious. I thought I was so streetwise until I was told later by a mate of mine who worked in his drag venue (we got talking as she was wearing the same black nail varnish as I – this was before punks, goths etc. so this was considered outrageous at the time, and she was actually saving up for the op and was turning tricks on the side) that he really did think I was good in the show, and would probably was intending to give me a job (presumably without sleeping with him). However I would not have been able to do the routines and you win some, you lose some. I didn't fancy him, but I did like him, so I bought him a drink anyway, which he graciously accepted.

I was in Gerry's one night, when 'The Godfather', as they called him in Soho circles (the elder statesman of the family who owned the club) sent one of his boys over to summon me to his table. I thought he wanted to sleep with me and asked the actor known as 'Brian With The Beard', who ran the gaff, for the key to the ladies', and planned my escape out the window. Dee, his missus, had it, and she was deep in conference with some old geezer in the corner – and anyway, the windows had bars on. By the time I went over to his table, I was terrified.

He said in a quiet soothing voice, "Do you know you are shaking? I'm not trying to fuck you, I just wanted to say you're good in the show and buy you a drink!"

Barry and his company of henchmen thought it was hilarious. Sabena was still shaking. However, he turned out to be OK.

After I left the club, and before it became a proper knocking shop again (not under this management), Barry left, and it was taken over by these Maltese people. Most of them were very nice, except one of their hangers-on who thought he was 'Everybody's Self', as they say in Liverpool. He was in the Swiss Tavern one night (now a lovely gay bar called Comptons), and I had to remind him that the Maltese for please and thank you was 'grazzi', and I assured him these words would be understood if he bothered to use them – I was very brave in those days.

I did one day in the new club, and that was more than enough. This consisted of chatting up men with your top off until they bought you an expensive drink. I apparently made them loads of money (always did have the gift of the gab), and they offered me a job. I said I was grateful but there was going to be some point at which I get a slap because I won't, or I slap one of them for going too far, so they kindly took me out the side door (through the dirty cinema), gave me a bonus and we called it a day!

I was going to run a café in Soho with his backing (just a place to do business – no drugs, guns, turning tricks on the premises). We'd planned it all, then the whole family got banged up for their usual business – running brothels. Even the women got nicked. So that was the end of my cafe.

Another thing that happened at Gerry's club was bumping into Joss Ackland, who knew me from the King's Head. He was in 'Evita' at the time and I managed to get myself smuggled in past the stage door and watched from the wings! I was not averse to sneaking into theatres in the West End. I had a boyfriend who was head flyman, or dayman or whatever they were called at the time, in one of the West End theatres. There was a set on stage that was supposed to be a boy's dormitory, so we got busy in one of the beds. We fell asleep and had to be woken up in the morning by the day staff.

In between all this naughtiness, and striving to get an Equity card (the reason I started at the club in the first place), I was still jumping up and down at demos. I went to Ireland (Dublin and Belfast) by ferry but missed the duty free. On the way back, these lads thought I was going to kick off (I'd obviously had a few) and offered me some of theirs. By the time I got back to the Swiss I was stocious and Bob put me to bed upstairs. My chatting up these lads was a bit of a ploy – not to get a drink, but so that I was not searched by customs. The Republican literature in my rucksack was not exactly legal at that time, although it probably is now I'm sure, but then it was certainly contentious. I had already been questioned by the Garda, because of the company I was keeping. I discovered it was best to remember not to use someone's nickname if you don't know why they are called Ozzie (he had gone to Australia to escape custody).

The people I went to see took me to the Divas flats in the Falls Road – not a place to be wandering about with a cockney accent. They said, "Keep your gob shut and do that shite impression of a Belfast accent, if you have to open it! They won't know where the fuck you are from with any luck!"

It was all a ploy to see how brave I was, and if I could be trusted. I understand the Divas was pulled down soon after that, not before time – the people were lovely though, consisting of friendly criminals like the Irish reprobates I was used to in London.

I continued working at the Hope and Anchor for a while. I once threw Billy Connolly out of the cellar bar – he actually said, "Do you know who I am?"

One of the boys said, "Yes! You're just another drunk who is drinking up and going home!"

Being a big fan of his, I would like to think he said it as an intelligent parody of minor celebs, rather than a remark he thought would make any difference to us. The latter was a ploy tried by Mandy Smith (married to Bill Wyman for a while), who was serious – the bouncer in question did know who she was and slung her out for that reason.

At the Hope and Anchor, it was common practice for people to help themselves to drinks and pay the next morning. The bloke serving afters said there were some people he wanted to get rid of, so I helped myself upstairs, wrote it down, and paid the next morning. The dopey article behind the bar was not paying attention when I pointed out I was paying my bar bill. John called me into the office and sacked me. I was very upset! Mick said it was because his tills were short, because someone was nicking. We both knew who it was, but didn't want to grass her up. He sacked Mick as well, but took him back on later! I still like John and Sue though and one day I'll give them back their cookbook I borrowed about 35 years ago!

CHAPTER SEVEN
Up the Passage!

When I got back from the holiday camp, Mick had some problem with a woman called Sian who owed him some money. Sian had a big smack problem and was living in a squat with loads of other addicts. Although I liked some of the people that lived there, a bunch of junkies are not likely to be the most reliable people in the world. I had already had a couple of problems with people at the squat where she lived, but I'm a glutton for punishment. I suppose I always want to help.

I was round there one night and we were all smoking what I was told was some strong sensimilla. I assumed it was skunk, then it really started to knock my head off and I started to feel seriously woozy and queasy. Then I realised. I was saying to myself in my head, "Sabena, you're an idiot, you're in a house full of junkies and you think they're smoking dope?"

Smoking smack is not an experience I wish to repeat, even by accident. I was ill for days. The time before that, I'd been round there drinking after the pub and, unbeknownst to me, this young girl goes off and jacks up in the lav. I was dying for a piss (believe me, you would rather pee in the street) when I found the silly cow on the floor turning blue with the works still in her arm. I managed to get her to some kind of consciousness. As I was only pissed and had not partaken in anything illegal, I got everyone to bugger off with their gear and a neighbour called an ambulance for me. I must have carried the daft bugger round that street for about 20 miles, saying "Don't you dare die on me!"

They'd told me to keep her awake. The neighbours might have given me a hard time but the ambulance man said I'd done well! I don't know what happened to her but I did ring the hospital, and found out she survived (that was all they could say).

Anyway Sian had got herself in a bad way, and was in hospital, very ill with abscesses on her arms from jacking up. Mick had rescued a load of books from the squat that were quite valuable, before the other inhabitants of the squat flogged them for scag. When Sian came out of hospital Mick refused to give her back her books until she paid him back the money she had borrowed. Unbeknown to us, Sian was turning tricks 'up the Cross' and picked up a copper (I am not explaining how I know this, but let us say Mick and I received some inside info a lot later on). The copper asked where she got the smack she's full off, and she decided to get back at Mick by giving his name as her smack dealer (which he absolutely was not).

Later on Mike Khan was round my place and he and Mick were playing cards all night, whilst drinking enormous amounts of alcohol. I'd just travelled from Norfolk and was asleep and sober. At six in the morning I was awoken by a bang on the door, so I opened the Victorian sash window and yelled "What do you want?" (as you do). This copper asked me if this was my car. I knew straight away no-one in council flats in London owns an expensive new car. By the time I'd convinced the other two we were about to be raided, the Old Bill had bashed in both doors. All they found was a bit of dope and a bit of speed, but they arrested Mick for supplying anyway. It was obvious they expected to find something else but we did not know what. They kept asking if there was any more, but there wasn't. Mike refused to give his last name (Police in Islington were still renowned for their racism), so some bright spark thought I looked vulnerable, knew it was my flat and demanded Mike's last name otherwise he would do me for allowing drugs to be sold on my premises. I told him not to bother as I would just complain to his superior for harassment. I further pointed out that I could not be complicit as I had got back from Caister Holiday Camp late last night, where I had been for seven months. A more experienced DC talked him out of it.

Eventually, they realised there was nothing else to find and left. It was not until later we found out they were looking for Class As – then their bad behaviour began to make sense. Unfortunately, after Mike made an official complaint (they were trying to bully him into a confession and he was the only one there who did not even smoke dope), I got arrested in Liverpool at a football match (West Ham versus Liverpool if anyone is interested), and ended up in custody for a while. I have no criminal record and do not wish to relive the experience, or blame anyone, so I won't be expanding on this subject.

After a while Tony Crosby, who played guitar with Mike Khan's band, moved into the bedroom. We had been lovers but at this point we were just good mates. Unlike hundreds of other people who had dossed on my floor, he actually gave me some money towards his keep, as he had worked behind the bar at the Hope with Mick and I. Crosby was difficult at times – Mick and I were both big drinkers, and so were most of our friends, so we didn't really take on board how much of a problem he had with it. Now I look back, it was obvious. The three of us spent a lot of time together and we had some brilliant times. Underneath it all Tony could be a lovely man and a really caring person. He was also was an amazing and talented guitarist – he had some brilliant chances but always seemed to always cock up everything. At times he had had the chance of going on tour with John Otway and doing gigs with Ozzy Osborne.

Now I look back, it was usually his drinking that messed it up. He used to start all sorts of fights when he'd had a few, to the point where I punched him so hard once that I nearly knocked him out (well... he was unconscious for a couple of minutes). He had disappeared from the cellar bar, and was trying to pretend the nasty fight he had just caused was nothing to do with him. I found him sweeping behind the bar upstairs, when I pointed out the error of his ways he went for me, and I completely lost it with him and clonked him one. I did forgive him, yet again, because I knew he had a lot of demons. I think it was the drink that led to our final falling out. We were all completely out of it (Mick and I, Tony and his girlfriend from New Zealand he had moved in) the night before and not much more compos mentis by the morning. In the haze I realised, in the booze and drug induced blur, that I had seen Crosby go to Mick's trousers and take some money out. When Mick and I had fully woken up later I got him to check his pockets. There was a tenner missing (a lot of money then, but that isn't the point). Eventually Crosby admitted it and I asked him to leave. It's water under the bridge now, but at the time I could not forgive him. "And take that bloody air rifle Spider was taking potshots at the neighbours with!"

He had also upset Mike Khan (not a good idea – he made a good and loyal friend but a dangerous enemy), so he buggered off back to Nottingham, where amazingly he is apparently still alive. His girlfriend stayed on with me for a while then went back to Auckland. He will turn up briefly later!

I wonder on reflection if Tony's behaviour was contributory to getting sacked from the Hope, or if I just got on their tits (it could have been the noisy encounter I had with the a certain gentleman from a certain reggae band in the ladies' toilet, halfway up the stairs, audible to anyone wishing to go between bars... when he was supposed to be on stage and I was supposed to be behind the bar... nobody could have missed the racket, apparently). Anyway, I needed to move on.

After the club I got quite a lot of door work because people had seen me work the door at the Hope. I worked for a gay pub. Once the women realised I was neither anti-lesbian or likely to nick their girlfriend we got on fine – don't think a bunch of gay women, all off their heads on all sorts, easy to control – they have more to prove in a punch-up!

I did a bit for Harvey Goldsmith (I was the only woman who worked that particular door – I don't miss it). I got introduced to Screaming Lord Sutch at the Dublin Castle or some such gig and ended up doing the door for him (it was one of Dave's gigs where I met Cynthia Payne – nice woman, never did get her to sign her book for me). I even did a stint for 'Fatty' Farlowe (as people in Islington called him), also known as Chris Farlowe, in his cocktail bar. We used to argue politics, and although he sells Nazi memorabilia, he's a very intelligent man and not the racist people think he is. I was sorry when this particular venture of his went tits up – I suppose it was 'Out of Time'! (Yes very funny.)

He's very slim these days! It was at Farlowe's I used to drink with Arthur Mullard – it was around the time when he and Hilda Baker did that daft song from 'Grease'. We used to walk around Islington sitting on park benches and he used to tell me anecdotes about his early days in the business. I wish I had written them down. He wanted me to accompany him to a couple of places, so he had a young lady on his arm to show off – I said alright, but no hanky-panky. We went out to a couple of places with us both dressed up to the nines and had a great time. Then I went off somewhere for a while, came back and he'd died – I was very sad.

I needed something to keep the wolf from the door, so I got a job in a bar near Camden Passage I liked. The couple who ran it were lovely and I got to know them well later, but the brewery wages were so poor, for so many hours I could not pay the rent. I ended up getting to know them better. Later, they ended up running quite a good drag house at the end of the market. Then I got a job in the snooker rooms with a geezer called Alan, whose wife was nice but he was well pervy (too touchy-feely for my liking) and made it obvious he expected me to sleep with him – creepy old git! Trying it on was one thing, but he would not take no for an answer. So I got a job at another pub, just up the road from the Angel, and had some great times working at this next madhouse. The governor (Guvvy) and I are still mates!

Firstly, have you ever seen the bit in Fools and Horses where they are all wearing Pringle jumpers? I did not see this until a long time after it was first shown, but when I did I rolled about the floor laughing. The people with me at the time said, "It's not *that* funny – is she on one?"

I said, "It is if you've seen it for real!"

Yes, everyone in the bar was wearing a so-called Pringle (until they fell apart) or an angora (they shrunk). Or there were the Cartier watches (the gold metal came off) or the Rolex (the pretend diamond was slightly off-kilter). We won't talk about the funny money, the passports or any of that, but even if we did all the perpetrators of these misdemeanours have been banged up for them – not that I knew any of them in the first place, Your Honour.

My husband Marc bought a 'Rolex' years later, for about a fiver, and some idiot in the Cock at Highbury wanted to buy it for thousands. Marc was very well-behaved, and said it wasn't for sale, but he was understandably tempted when this idiot was waving the money in his face aggressively, demanding to buy it.

There were some absolutely brilliant times working with Guvvy and the crew. His girlfriend of the moment did not seem to do much but drink huge quantities of wine, whilst perched on a barstool – not that I can preach about the boozing, mind you I didn't start as soon as I got up... in fact, not until I'd finished work, mind you she didn't do any work. I had nothing against her particularly, but when she buggered off with someone else, it was no great loss to any of us – particularly Guvvy. I started doing food as well as my bar duties. I worked with an Australian girl, Lisa (nicknamed 'Budgie' because she ate like a bird). My family (Marc and our two kids) and I went to stay with her in Perth – more about Oz later.

Bill the Brush – he used a paintbrush to clean ashtrays – was always on about the fact that his missus was so much younger than he. After all this boasting, when she turned up we expected some model. Nice enough girl, but apart from her weight problem, she was no oil painting bless her. I can't remember what happened to Bill but he was replaced by Guvvy's old mate Clarkey (or sometimes Cluckles if you wanted a favour), who 'moaned for England'.

My first encounter with Clarkey was over the phone. Guvvy got me to talk dirty to him for a laugh, but we ended up ignoring all that and having a proper intelligent conversation, much to Guvvy's annoyance. The main target for Clarkey's moaning was the governor's son, who he normally addressed as 'That Little Fucker', as in "That little fucker has put my fucking bar float in that fucking fruit machine again!"

The young gentleman in question did a brilliant impression of a phone conversation between Clarkey – East End Cockney and Derek (the governor of the next pub up) – Yorkshire. Apart from the brilliant and accurate impressions, the main source of amusement was that neither of them could speak a sentence without a very liberal use of the F-word. As in, "Allo! It's fucking Clarkey, what d'you fucking want?"

"'Ellow, it's fucking Derek 'ere, t'fucking beooewery fucking forgot t'fucking ale order a-fucking-gain, can I borrow some fucking beer?"

And so on. Clarkey took up with a lovely lady called Hettie (eh – glottal-stop – ee), who used to be a gangster's moll. 'Ettie used to tell him off for swearing. She came and had a drink one lunch time when Clarkey was working behind the bar and had promised her he would be on his best behaviour. He spent the whole lunchtime minding his Ps and Qs – not an F word. All of a sudden, while counting the money (the little fucker had been at it again), he blurted out, "If that fucking till's right, my prick's a bloater!"

Of course we all burst out laughing while 'Ettie gave him an ear bashing, which didn't help. Of course it was excusable under the circumstances.

Guvvy, Cluckles, Budgie and I made a splendid team though and had lots of laughs. I remember we had a problem with the plumbing and I sent Budgie over to the Steam Passage to borrow a monkey wrench to turn off the stopcock. It would seem even Aussie girls who have been in charge of packs of huge miners in the diamond mines have trouble with English plumbing terms. The Governor couldn't work out what a monkey cock was – that girl had cock on the brain, she was almost as bad as I was for running about with naughty villains. The Tartan Tortoise (called so because he was London's slowest Scottish cleaner) sorted it out in the end. We used to joke about this bank robber she had been going out with for a while, dubbed 'Mr Spam-Head' (he was bald). She reckoned he was crying all over the frozen food because he was so heartbroken at her finding another lover!

One afternoon Guvvy caught me creeping up the stairs to the then empty function room with Peter the Painter, and whilst in the middle of very enjoyable and horny blowjob and various other bits of naughtiness (so I enjoyed it as much as he did), I realised all the staff and half the customers were watching through the glass in the door! With Guvvy giving a running commentary (probably as if it were a horse race, knowing him).

Later on I used the function room to start a very successful catering business. I did an Irish wedding there – I put a load of shamrocks all over the shop and did some traditional Irish stuff. It wasn't the Gresham Ballroom (the notorious Irish club at the end of Holloway Road), on a Saturday night, but with a bit of 'Diddly-Dah' music, as they call it in London, it worked out really well. I went on to do loads of weddings and parties in unused function rooms at various pubs and even a bar mitzvah in Stoke Newington. I did a deal for some wholesale Kosher food with Brewer and Spitzer and made it a real traditional buffet. They were so knocked out I got a hundred pounds extra – a lot of dosh in those days.

It was here that I met my lovely friend Michael the artist, whose professional name was Flick. One of his paintings still hangs on our bedroom wall. I think he was responsible for the nickname 'Doggie' being bestowed upon me (although *he* used to call me the 'Old Splosher').

Flick was manager at Robert Carriers restaurant up the road. During his breaks, and when I wasn't working, he and I liked to sit by the stairs leading up to the gents. Our favourite pastime was to make lewd, personal, frank and sometimes downright catty comments about the various bits of anatomy of the 'passing trade'. Whether or not one or both of us had actually sampled the eye candy on display did not detract us from the blatancy of our comments, often within earshot of the whole pub. This practice got us referred to as a pair of old dogs (hence my nickname).

Naturally Flick referred to all the men as 'she' – whether they were camp or not had nothing to do with it. Flick's best drinking pal Humphrey was maitre d' at Fredericks, a long established restaurant, and the only place that would even be close to competition – the old 'Carrier Bag' (as he was dubbed by Guvvy) being one of the most eminent telly-chefs at the time.

Humphrey knew the place well so marched everywhere at breakneck speed, despite his blindness. As he passed the pub, as if on a mission, Guvvy would demand in his best upper class army colonel accent "*Humphrey!*" and Humphrey would reply "*Sir!*" while saluting in the general direction of the third floor window from whence the racket came. The whole Passage enjoyed this ritual – especially the stallholders who were just setting up in the gentleness of the Islington early morning, before rush-hour's hell broke loose.

His only real disability was exaggeration. According to Humphrey, who undoubtedly by his accent went to one of the better public schools, he was related to every bit of royalty and aristocracy you've never heard of. Michael used to say, "She's got the pedigree of Wobbly Bobbly's dog!" (This extraordinary creature looked as if it was made from several kits of different breeds, as if the mechanic had got the boxes mixed up – the dog wasn't much better).

Of course this nonsense of Humphrey's that impressed no-one only made him more endearing. Despite his pretences at aloofness, Humphrey was partial to a good conversation, and even more partial to an afternoon shag.

The couple I had worked for previously were now regular customers at Guvvy's pub – their pub being just round the corner. Michael had dubbed her Mrs Badgers some while back, as she nagged people a lot. They were (she and her husband) by this time formerly known as 'The Badgers'. Even their pub was nicknamed the Badgers' locally, although its real name escapes me. Although they were disappointed I was not working for them they were mates with Guvvy and delighted I had found a job I enjoyed.

At lunchtimes, 'Mad Jack' often used to collect the dirty plates, so Guvvy used to give him a pint now and again, but he did it because he liked me and I liked him. This was fortunate because he was not called Mad Jack for nothing and, if Mad Jack got a cob on, he could seriously damage everything and everybody in the pub, causing complete havoc in a matter of minutes – so he was not a person to upset. Rumour has it that his missus upset him, so he decided she needed a bath with a hairdryer, but that may just be a rumour.

I'd only been working there for a couple of days when three brothers and a couple of their sons came in. Guvvy said to me, "You want to be careful of this lot, they are right naughty boys!"

I walked up to the bar and the eldest brother said, "Hello Sabena, what you doing working for this reprobate? How's your granddad getting on?"

Guvvy slapped himself on the head and said to me quietly, "I should have fucking known!"

He soon realised there were very few people in Islington I didn't know, especially of the naughty variety! One lady who I got on well with used to chat to me and buy me drinks. "You want to be careful of her!" Guvvy said.

"They call her the 'Black Widow' – she's done time for murder."

I said, "What's that got to do with me? I ain't gonna marry her – why, do you think she fancies me? I thought she liked boys?"

Guvvy said, "She does... for breakfast!"

Her latest was my greengrocer, albeit a part-time hard case himself. I was still doing weights, from time to time, and still doing a bit of boxing training with Mike Khan. As one customer put it, "The geezer delivers two huge sack of spuds, struggles to the bottom of the stairs from his van with them on his little handcart and she slings one on each shoulder and runs up three flights of stairs with them!" The silly bugger blew himself up making some bomb for some reason or another – shame, I liked him. The place was absolutely full of villains, and therefore awash with coke (I got given so much of the stuff for nothing, so I decided to knock it on the head in the end, before I developed a serious habit, but I still smoked a lot of dope and drank a lot).

Clarkey used to do a little song and dance to the Hokey Cokey – "You stick a bit up here..." (pretending to snort coke off his thumb), "a bit up there...!"

There was also the customer who was rumoured to have been one of the Essex boys. Another gentleman of the gangster ilk was drinking with Guvvy, and they were whispering like conspiring schoolgirls. "Go on, give her the keys, she's alright!"

So Guvvy asked me to get something from the boot of this bloke's car, under the spare wheel. When I lift up the cover, there's a bloody great shotgun. So I get whatever he was asking for and put it back as it was, making sure I didn't touch the gun. I calmly give him whatever it was, and he asked, "Everything alright?"

And I said, "Yep!" – handing him the small object, whatever it was, and throwing my eyes in the air like they're a daft pair of kids. His mate loved it! Another mate sold my present old man a red beamer a lot later (well, he was on holiday at Her Majesty's pleasure so had little use for it and his missus didn't drive). Policemen do look silly when they stop someone and say, "Have you always been that colour sir?" or "Oh, er, is this your car sir?" ("So you're not banged up in the Ville awaiting sentence then?")!

The pub was also frequented by another naughty mate of Guvvy's that I pulled eventually. I used to know him from Soho, he'd been a big noise in the West End bars (for gangster activities) around Soho and turned up later briefly when I worked for the Jobcentre. There I was, a 'respectable' civil servant at a conference to discuss helping long-term unemployed people back to work. Suddenly into the room I heard this booming voice I recognised.

"It can't be!" I thought to myself. When I realised it was I decided not to let on I knew this villain, let alone that we were lovers. After all, it must be a blag if someone with his criminal history was in a large government building requiring security clearance.

However he did not behave with such caution and gave me a big smacker, and started talking (in excruciating detail) about when I was a stripper and how one of the other girls he fancied had an inordinate amount of dark pubic hair. Then it transpired the Department of Work & Pensions were well aware of his record and he's running a unit for 'NACRO', helping ex-cons get work. He had to explain when he saw the look of concern on my face – he knew I wondered what I was being roped into. He starts his presentations explaining that he has spent half his life in prison and he will never, ever get that wasted time back again.

Sometime later Marc (my current husband) and I went to see Guvvy. We met him in a North London pub that was opened when it should not have been (pubs then were supposed to close in the afternoon). We were greeted by a white gentleman with a scar that went from his ear to his mouth. He said, "Yes, who are you?" as if we'd both shat in his shoe.

Marc said nonchalantly, "We're with him!" – pointing back to Guvvy.

"Sorry! Sorry!" the man apologised in almost Uriah Heep manner, as if he had made some serious faux pas, and gave Guvvy a hero's welcome. When we got in the pub there was more coke than Bogota. In fact, apparently in the Gents there was a queue for the window-sill. Also someone had recently done a warehouse so everyone on the manor had a set of these particular doors – same pattern, same colour. One old boy had two doors leaned up against the wall behind him in the pub, ready to put in his van.

"I know you!" said an evil looking large black gentleman who was two of Marc wrapped together. I knew him too.

"Aw gawd!" I thought, remembering he was one of my customers from the Jobcentre who had done time for murder. "Yes I know your face from somewhere!" I lied.

"You interviewed me at the Jobcentre!" he interrupted. "You was right nice to me, you got me a job, would you and your man like a drink?"

"Err, yes please! Err, yes I remember you!" I backtracked. "Good job I was nice to you, eh?"

I let the joke hang in the air, looking up at him even though we were both seated. At the bar was a huge, light-ish skinned black fella I recognised from the old days. "I understand you used to look after this reprobate!" he said to Marc, shaking his hand. "I'm looking after him now, don't you worry – he's in good hands!"

He spoke in broad gangster cockney (we lived in Norfolk by then). "Good!" said Marc authoritatively, delighted at being mistaken for a minder-come-henchman. It was a delightful afternoon, and we got given so much coke Marc was really off his head – so much so that I made him swap seats so he did not have his back to the door, just in case a row broke out, but no violence was even threatened! At least not audibly.

We enjoyed another afternoon later on with Guvvy, after we'd moved away from the insanity of North London. We were in this pub just off the main drag in Camden, so all the 'oysters' ('hoisters' – shoplifters, although actually 'oysters' suits the translucent nature of an unhealthy addict's skin colour) would wander in with whatever they had nicked from the local shops to sell for a bag of smack. At that time a bag was fifteen quid, so whether it was a push bike or a pair of trousers it was a fiver. Drinking at the bar was a twenty-handed round of North London's most notable gangsters. Suddenly two coppers (in what they called plain clothes) appeared at the door. As soon as they did, the whole pub erupted into 'Clanger'.

If you have not seen 'The Clangers', they only communicate in a high-pitched whistle. For the twenty minutes they chanced their arm, no-one in the pub spoke. After a while you not only understand what's occurring, but you become fluent. Someone in the corner was quietly humming the theme to 'Z-Cars'.

Then one plod said to the other, "What's the fucking point?"

The other one yelled out, "You're all a bunch of bastards, you're all scum anyway!" and off they went, to a chorus of the 'Laurel and Hardy' exit tune. Almost immediately, two junkies came in with a wide screen TV and the keys to a Range Rover (God only knows where those two items are now).

Much later when Marc and I were living in Norfolk we had a brief lunch with Flick. He was very thin, very ill and obviously dying, but I did not want to visit him when he got worse and he would not have wanted me to see him like that! Goodbye dear friend – I will always miss you!

CHAPTER EIGHT
Silly Bollocks

It was while I was working in this pub that I met my first husband. He was caretaking the rundown pub up the road. I started knocking about with his barman at first, and one night when he'd stood me up I chatted up Tony. As his barman had dyed blonde hair and there were only the two of them living in the pub, the local grapevine put two and two together and made five and assumed they were two gay fellas. Guvvy nicknamed Tony 'Pluto' – skinny with big feet and daft I suppose, but eventually he joined everyone else, and called him 'Silly Bollocks'. The reason for this will become apparent. It wasn't quite love at first sight, but I did fall for Tony, big time.

Of course I suppose I thought I had found my 'soulmate'. We got married after we finished at the pub at the Angel. Flick (Michael) borrowed a 'Rolls' to take me to the Registry Office, and apart from the odd punch up (nothing to do with Silly Bollocks), the wedding went OK.

Although we got on fine for a while, I should have known from the start that apparently he had all the psychological traits. For a start he was insanely jealous (he once accused me of shagging some poor old geezer of about eighty who said hello to me in the street, who had been a customer in Keith's pub). He also had a ridiculous drink problem, to the tune of a case of large bottles of Skol Special and a bottle of brandy a day. The other clue was that he had been caretaking difficult pubs for a while. He said he got paid to work on the security side, because he could do a bit of boxing. Usually if you work under a security contract, they try you out in a few shit-holes and then give you a rough but profitable pub to make a go of, instead of one that was being kept open for the licence. Well it was true enough, for a little skinny fella he could have a row, and as I had been taught a bit of boxing I could see he also had some idea. This turned out to be about the most truthful thing about him.

He was an inveterate liar and a habitual wife beater, but I was naïve and fell in love with a man I thought was a romantic, who obviously adored me. In fact he was a sexist control freak who was probably psychopathic. Even when he first hit me, I was naïve enough to believe him when he said would not happen again. Unfortunately by the time it did, we were married.

People caught in a circle of domestic violence are difficult for outsiders to understand. I was very young and vulnerable, emotionally. I assumed anyone I confided in, including my parents, would have a 'you made your bed, now lie in it' approach – especially as most of my previous boyfriends had harboured some sort of conflict with the Old Bill. What with his constant lies, his insistence that it was my fault and that I drove him to it, and my general lack of confidence, it was an easy spiral to be brainwashed into.

Although I was in this seemingly inescapable cycle of violence, I had realised even then, in the back of my mind, I had to get out before he killed me. Subconsciously, I began plotting my exit. Daytimes were not so bad, as he went out drinking and left me to run the pub. This was something I found I was good at. The customers generally preferred me to him (of course that was my fault as well, as I must have turned them against him and I probably made them feel sorry for me). The fact that my husband was regularly beating me up was not something I ever spoke about, although it must have been obvious what was 'occurring' as Guvvy would say. I generally sported at least the remains of a shiner – even the company's roughest pubs were not that rough (some of the pubs we ran together I went back to run on my own, later).

Eventually his lies got exposed one by one. Gradually, it dawned on me that everything he blathered about that I thought might be a bit suspect turned out to be totally Pinocchio. Even Pam Ayres' 'Little Lawrence Greenaway' would have considered he had a diabolical liberty!

For instance, I noticed down in the cellar two bottles of gin had been bought in (they bore a non-brewery mark on them), so I told him, but he was having none of it. I realised he did not know how to tell the difference, but

Mister 'You don't know what you are talking about, mere woman' regretted this. Unfortunately the stock-taker proved me right, and when I remonstrated that they were already in the cellar when I arrived and I had assumed the last stock-taker would have made a note, he said he *was* the last stock-taker and they were not in the cellar then. Before I argued in S.B.'s defence he told me he had bad stocks before – due to his drinking, he expected.

Of course with that information in mind, and with this daft idea that he would stop drinking so much when we were married, I covered his drinking by buying in Martini. This was the preferred drink of our very own gang of ageing villains (usually about 30 of them at a time), who frequented the bar at lunchtime, thereby avoiding any enemies they may have made when younger and more handy. S.B. also managed to upset them with his lack of tact. One of the not so bright petty criminals, loitering with the aforementioned naughty granddads, had just been paid for some nefarious deed with some funny-money. Having spotted it straight away I entrusted 'His Wobbliness' (who appeared reasonably sober) with the task of returning the homemade note with some tactful advice. Instead of seizing upon this chance to usurp his position as 'the guv'nor', he gobbed off in front of the others and all hell broke loose (although they probably knew the scumbag who had been shafted by anyway, and could have sorted it out if S.B. hadn't made such a big fuss). This meant that the victim of this piece of shit on his own doorstep had to show bravado in front of the others, forcing him to vow to go and "Sort it out with the bastard!"

The resulting altercation, it transpired, contributed to his next stretch. A little nous on the part of S.B. could have avoided all this shite!

Then there was the Silly Billy incident. He was a local character, and the nickname was not meant to be vindictive but descriptive of the effect of a combination his learning disability and drink problem – in harsh London vernacular it was almost sympathetic. He would often appear at lunchtimes, as he knew he would get spoiled with drinks (one of the main players in the company had a son with a similar situation). So he rocked up when he knew the old boys would be in the pub. This suited me as, although Silly Billy was barred from most places, this lot promised to keep him in order. So I said he could stay as long as he didn't do anything naughty (like getting his old man out and whacking it on the bar, as was his wont).

One day I thought he had decided to break the rule without apparent encouragement or enough warning so they could restrain him (I was serving someone who fortunately could not see). Out comes his old man and he slaps it on the bar with a gleeful "Rollop!" – he could not pronounce W. One or two people started laughing. It was not a pretty sight, and despite the fact that his Hampton was on the huge side, I was not impressed in any sort of way.

S.B. seemed to relinquish his 'Guv'nor' status and did a disappearing act. So I reluctantly banned Billy with surprisingly little protest, despite upsetting the company, who had tried to stop him displaying the beast. The whole thing made sense when one of the lads told me Silly Bollocks had not only encouraged him, but had opened a bloody book on Billy doing his party trick! Eventually it dawned on me that Tony wasn't the wonderfully competent publican, respected by the brewery, he had made himself out to be. He was just a child who had not grown up who wanted to be 'in charge'.

The pub, only opened to avoid re-application of the licence, had been a millstone round the brewery's neck for a long time, but in the end we did quite well. I was doing much better than the brewery realised on the food (well, they never asked), and I hoped we would end up with the pub long-term, but of course they already had a couple to take over when it was done up.

S.B. had a dog called Hutch, named after some Chelsea player. I could never understand his obsession with football. He was a lousy footballer himself, and had, by all accounts, never been sporty himself in any way. Although admittedly I had been quite a good customer of the Shed myself as an on/off supporter of West Ham. I loved all the excitement of the live match, even though I wasn't going to kill everybody if West Ham lost (last time I saw West Ham, Trevor Brooking was still playing, instead of boring the shit out of me on the telly). S.B. dragged me along to the Chelsea matches. I began wondering about the 'big man's' lack of courage – after all it was me who went up to Ken Bates and all the players to get their autographs at the end of a charity match (Ken Bates gave my T-shirt a disapproving look – it was one Madness had given me with 'Fuck Art Let's Dance!' written on it). It dawned on me as I started to fall out of love with him, apart from the inane violence, he was not very brave or particularly capable of much.

I already knew he wasn't the sharpest knife in the box. Later a work colleague at the Jobcentre said S.B. used violence because he was terrified of me. I was much brighter and stronger than he was.

Anyway, back to my lovely dog Hutch. He was mainly shoved onto the roof instead of being walked, and S.B. tried to hide his previous neglect of the poor thing. I started to walk him twice daily, fed him proper food and made sure he was not left out in the cold in his own shit (I cleared all that up as well). Naturally he became a nicer better behaved dog when I was there to look after him instead of this feral beast S.B. had let him had become. Mind you, I found out later he only bit in retaliation for violence, so the only person he ever bit was S.B.

Sometimes I wondered who was the most grown-up – the dog or S.B.? Hutch was certainly more emotionally stable. We ran a series of other clapped out pubs. At least, I ran them and he got drunk somewhere else. One of them was an ugly pub in Walthamstow, surrounded on all sides by tower blocks, where the publican was so disliked by the locals, they had put scaffolding boards through all the windows. Any architect who places a pub on an estate, detached on all sides, ought to be made to live there! In fact all architects all should be made to live in their own monstrosities.

Eventually, I found out who smashed it up and why. A little birdie told me a couple of black fellas he had barred for no reason were responsible. I only met the old governor once, but he was a blatant racist, which did not go down well with either the locals, or me. So I kept this little snippet of info under-me-hat. Before my little 'conflab' with the local mafia we were regularly broken into, so it was bedlam with the alarm going off and the dog running up and down the stairs, but this stopped and it became a nice pub you could bring your Granny to.

After the allotted eight months of me sorting out the trouble I asked the area manger if we could take it over. He said, cutting through the crap, "When you've ditched this drunken idiot, I've always got a job for you!"

I realised then that they were just using S.B. and had no intention of giving him a permanent job. This was further confirmed when, respectably married, we went for an interview for a pub in Hounslow, where he came from and wanted to go back to. I wasn't keen, since I had escaped from the boredom of South West London once, but I went along anyway (to dutifully support my husband I suppose). However, he barely said a word when we got there and for all his 'I'm the boss' crap, he left the talking to me. I recognised the bloke doing the interviews vaguely (another area manager apparently), and he kept looking at me whilst going through copies of marriage certificates. I suspect he thought I had been married to some other no-hoper.

Suddenly it dawned on me who he was. I did not explain to him why I looked familiar – there was no point. Anyway, S.B. blamed me for losing the pub. He obviously could not remember the head bar person, who was respected enough by one of his training managers to run his cellar for him. Our first meeting was when I was asked to prove I could drag a full barrel across a cellar – yes, he was that sexist dickhead!

I made loads of suggestions at the interview, all of which the couple who *were* given the pub implemented on instruction from the brewery. Obviously they liked my ideas, as no-one in the brewery seemed to have any of their own. All these pubs were a nightmare until we settled down the local hooligans and stopped them coming in and causing havoc (or just performing the kind of 'cabaret' you can live without). I suppose if we had worked together we would have been a good team, but S.B. could not bring himself to do anything that did not cause someone some kind of distress – it seemed to be his sole raison d'etre. Shame it took me so long to realise.

The best time I had with S.B. was when we were on holiday. My first visit to Amsterdam (one of his football hooligan mates had moved there with his Dutch wife, who was a diamond – his mate was OK as well, much brighter than S.B.). We went with a couple of younger friends, and while S.B. was trying to corrupt the lad into alcoholism, me and the girl saw the sights. As I was only in the company of women S.B. was unusually calm.

We also went to Spain (Majorca first and later the mainland) several times. Once with his older drunken mate Barry from the post office, and that was good fun too. S.B. and I stayed in El Arenal. It was a cheap package thing where they could change venue at the last minute. S.B. was mortified at first. Needless to S.B. had wanted to go back to nearby Magaluf, which one of his mates described as a shithole full of lager louts just like Tony. At great expense he took me there to show me how wonderful it was – and not only was I predictably unimpressed, but S.B., being more sober than usual, decided to settle for El Arenal. Even he had realised it had much more to offer.

After a while he got into the 'going to see the world about us, instead of drinking all day' idea and suggested we went to Seville. He was going to talk to some dozy travel rep – I said, "Don't bother with that – the bus is only sixpence!" We had to stand, but it did not matter, and we drove up the mountain in a bus that seemed to belong in a third world country and had a really good day. We went back on the cheap package holiday twice more. We also went to Fuengirola (he boasted he could speak a bit of Spanish... could he fuck, and his accent was awful – when he tried to say Fuengirola it sounded like 'furry goolies').

When I was working with Groundwell Farmers Theatre Group, I had met a lovely lady called Caroline. I didn't really understand then, but she had an on/off mental illness. She appeared out of nowhere with little plausible explanation, so I put her up in the flat when Mick and I lived together. When Mick and I had parted company, Caroline and he had a bit of a thing going and for a while she moved in with him. Well, I went off to live with S.B., Mick went off doing his own thing and got a flat of his own and suggested Caroline and the kids did the same. She had been living in a flat upstairs after the last tenants had left, and we didn't see her very often. The gas and electric had been left on, so we assumed it was still on and the council were rehousing her. But Caroline and the kids were still squatting upstairs, and neither of us realised how ill she was. Nor did we realise the gas and electricity was off, and no-one from the council had been to see her or the kids.

While I was running one of the pubs with S.B. the police turned up out of the blue. The older child was with her dad and the youngest child had died of hypothermia. Caroline had run out of money and was too ill to cope by herself. When I had last asked where the child was she just said it was upstairs with someone or other – this was the last conversation I had with her, and what she had told other people. The baby had been dead for some time when they found her. There was no other problem with the child – she had just died of the cold.

I'm truly, very sorry Caroline. I should have realised. I let you down badly!

The beatings from S.B. got worse. After one serious beating I decided to try and get a divorce. S.B. had had a lot to drink and some fisticuffs with another idiot in the pub had put him in one of his 'red mist' moods. I had already tried various strategies – fighting back (he would just hit harder), running away (he would just lock me in), pretending to be asleep (he would hit me until I woke up), and so on.

The more I told him he needed help, the more he blamed me, and to begin with I believed him. The amount of booze I was putting away at that time was not doing much for my mental health either. This time I felt myself going into unconsciousness as he hit me over and over again. Every time I got up he knocked me down again. I knew he was going to kill me soon if I did not do something, but I did not know who to turn to. I sloped into the kitchen and got a knife out the drawer and slashed at him as he came for me, cutting off the thumb of the hand he had put up to stop me. Oh yes, in case you were wondering, I was going for his neck, and intended to cut off his head if necessary.

The first time I got away, I went to Mike's and tried to get away by taking our area manager up on his offer. He gave me a pub to care-take just up from the Blind Beggar, on Bethnal Green Road ('tennis with mallets', as Guvvy would say). S.B. had tried to run this on his own before I met him and they had pulled him out for fear of his life (I did not know this at the time). As I was living in, he was unlikely to find me, or get it out of the brewery where I was.

Anyway I was in this pub, sitting on my own one night, and as I was just getting up to check the dopey barman had remembered to slam the door so it locked, this huge gorilla burst in wielding an axe, which he proceeded to impale in my bar as some kind of warning!

"You are wasting your time!" I said bravely, hoping he wasn't carrying a shank or a gun. "Whoever you are looking for probably went with the last guv'nor, and I've barred all the idiots he had in! Why don't you sit down, and

I'll pour you a nice drink. I'll get the brewery to sort out the bar tomorrow."

He had a quick double brandy, explained who he was looking for and why, and like the gentleman he obviously was, prised his axe out of my bar and took it home (he seemed to assume I had some vicious gorilla of a husband upstairs – thank God I didn't put him right). The brewery knew who he was but just got someone in to mend the hole in the bar (apparently you can still see the join – the bar is only short so it should be easy to find).

At another pub I ran, one of those London gangs (who people all pretend they have been mates with) had sent in their minions to get protection money. The last governor had been sending the brewery back water, as a bid to pay their boys protection. They had sent some brewery boys to 'look the business' in one pub I had run with S.B. – they were as much use as a chocolate teapot and caused more trouble than they sorted out, so I was not going to make that mistake again (although despite his usual ridiculous jealousy, S.B. had become mates with Mick the Gorilla, so we had hired him instead). This time I borrowed some friends of various naughty people I knew (mostly Mike Khan's). As most of them were either direct rivals, or working for rivals of the gentlemen who were bidding to become my minders (trying to take protection) – let's just say they were 'faces' I knew, and so did my adversaries.

These gentlemen happened to all meet up in my pub whilst taking their pet rottweilers for a walk (some of them were actually dogs). The gentlemen bidding to be my personal bouncers decided perhaps they did not want to 'protect' my pub after all. No bull and cow, just a bit of common sense and some help from my friends.

I was pretty sure the brewery were going to offer me the pub, but S.B. found me coming from Mike's one night after a gig, made me loads of promises and, encouraged by Mike, I went back to the flat with him. Of course the police were useless and even took his side on one occasion. By this time he had mysteriously stopped running pubs and moved back into my council flat permanently – my neighbour came up and apologised (when he wasn't there). She said he had made me out to be this violent harridan who was in the habit of waving knives about (as opposed to the little scared creature I had really become, who was frightened to say a word in case it provoked the next punch). Apparently she had seen him punch me in the street, and then she realised.

The next time I escaped I stayed at Flick's flat. At the same time Tony 'Towsens' (he was an Irish bloke who exaggerated, as in "There were towsens of them!") was staying there from time to time, running away from his violent Turkish missus (she was doolally and a half – most of the time when I saw her in the pub, she was talking to someone who wasn't there). Flick used to moan about being stuck being the nursemaid for two refugees, but we all had some good laughs, and I intended to go to the council as soon as my divorce came through. At that time Flick and I cooked dinner for Robert Carrier at Flick's flat – 'Ol' Carrier Bag', as Guvvy called him, was over from his place in France, where he now resided with his boyfriend. He was suitably impressed by the meal (lobster thermidor), and said although Flick was brilliant, I was a 'passable' chef. Sounded like a compliment to me... I think.

Flick did some framing work for the sweet Finbar McDonagh, who had a shop selling antique prints in the Passage (a delightful and clever bloke but a helpless drunk). S.B. being a creature of habit did not come to this part of Islington, so he did not know the streets as well as I, and if I saw him in the street I was able to get out of sight until he'd gone. After a while, I began pulling other men (I had not slept with anyone else since we had met up until then) – one of them was his boss at the Post Office, although I did not appreciate the irony at the time. He was someone I had fancied for a while and had known for a long time and I had made up my mind my marriage was over.

One night Mike Khan foolishly pointed out that I still loved S.B. and persuaded me to give it another go. He told me ring him up to meet at the flat. He then knocked S.B. all around the room and told him there would be a contract out on him, if he touched me again. Although it was not my idea, we both (Mike and I) foolishly thought this would work. It didn't.

When I went back I knew it was a mistake immediately. Despite still loving him, gawd knows why, I had enjoyed my newfound freedom and realised I was not useless on my own, and was perfectly capable of living without all this shit. S.B. had parted company with the brewery – this was never explained, he just said he'd had enough (I never mentioned to him that I had worked for them again but I told my area manager we were trying again – he just said he would keep the position open for six months).

We got a job in a pub by his beloved Chelsea's football ground working for the widow of Tibor Szakacz, the wrestler. She was a lovely lady, from Germany originally, and still had a strong accent. I struggled to cope with organising such a high standard of food in such a busy pub at first, but learned quite quickly – she was very tolerant and would say "You vin some ent you bloody vell loose some!"

S.B. was too busy behind the bar to do so much drinking, so things were better. Just as things seemed to be working, he decided he was fed up with the pub. Obviously all this work was eating into his drinking time. Our boss was quite upset when we left. I had become efficient in the kitchen and whatever he was or wasn't, S.B. was a good barman. Once we were not working S.B. had decided to have a 'little holiday', went and signed on and sat in the bloody pub all day. After a short time (about two weeks) I was bored stupid. I was bored with drinking, and we couldn't afford it anyway. Eventually I said, "We can't carry on like this, I'm going down the dole to get a job!"

The woman behind the bar (we were in the Alma in Newington Green) said they needed someone there, part-time, when can you start? I knew they were going to knock my wages off his dole money, but I had to escape, so it seemed like a good idea at the time.

He didn't like me being the breadwinner – so to speak – I did point out he could keep an eye on me as he was always in the pub. This didn't help. In the end it drove me ballistic and before he signed on again I told him I did not want to sit in the pub I worked in, watching him drink what little money we had left away, so I made good on my promise and went 'down the dole'!

They said I've got O-Levels and could come and work for them. I thought, "Well, it'll do for a bit." When the bloke who showed us around said I'd got a job for life, I was horrified. I wasn't even thirty years old!

So I started working for the Department of Stealth and Total Obscurity (as my Dad called it), at Kentish Town Jobcentre, replacing Laggi when he got promoted – he replaced Des Nilsen, when he got arrested (the serial killer). I did not find out I had been a serial killer's replacement, so to speak, until a lot later when the police turned up at Kentish Town Jobcentre to bully some poor man outside. The place was all glass and we could clearly see the police pushing him about, him being a major criminal and bang to rights (he had a learning difficulty and had nicked a pint of milk and a loaf of bread from Tesco). After witnessing this poor piece of racism, I just happened to be in the office of 'she who must be obeyed', complaining about their behaviour myself, when she told the police on the phone they were not welcome in the Jobcentre without permission. I noticed her playing with her pointed, deadly, but perfectly manicured finger nails. This was a sign she was nervous. When I asked what was wrong, she explained that it reminded her of the dreadful day when one of her staff was arrested as a serial killer. It all came out then. I found out he cooked his colleagues' curry in a pot he used to boil up the bones of his victims. He used to send my mate Smiffy out for a bottle of vodka each afternoon he was left on his own upstairs and he would drink it neat while doing everyone else's work.

I digress again....

My newfound independence and ability to pay the bills made me decide it was time cut my losses. The next time S.B. nearly killed me, I decided I had to take my chances (I knew that his threat to kill me and himself if I left again was serious, and he had already nearly killed me twice). I disappeared out of his life, never to return, although when he nearly strangled me, Mick the Gorilla was in the other room staying over. When I screamed "Help!" he understandably took no notice – he had heard it all before. I just kept laughing as if it didn't hurt, until he let go. A very good friend who had been an only occasional lover (unfortunately, I thought at the time), shifted my stuff to my Nan's old flat in Teddington while I knew S.B. was at work. My parents had kept it on for when my Dad worked in London, although they lived in Norfolk.

I had hidden things of mine in my flat's tiny loft (S.B. didn't notice they were missing), and decided not to come back for any reason. Unfortunately I had to leave my lovely dog as it was too complicated to take him. Sometime later he died of some kind of tumour, but I'm not so sure S.B. didn't have a hand in it. I had taken many beatings that were meant for the dog (and vice-versa). When I arrived at Mum and Dad's and saw a doctor in Norfolk, he looked at the mark on my neck where S.B. had strangled me and said, "My God, you are very lucky to be alive!"

I knew this!

CHAPTER NINE
The Marquess

For quite a while I made the impossible journey every day from Teddington to North London. The emotional turmoil began to take its toll and I began getting panic attacks for the first time. I was sure if S.B. caught up with me he would kill me and himself as he promised. I was just as terrified he would turn up at the Jobcentre and cause me a whole load of shit – maybe even lose me my job. I should have known he didn't have the bollocks to do either.

Instead he turned up at my Nan's old flat in Teddington two or three times, despite three court injunctions. I managed to get the police to arrest him before he hurt me each time, which is more than they ever did in Islington. Eventually I persuaded the council to re-house me somewhere where he could not find me. I was desperate by now. I knew there were empty places on the Marquess Estate, because no one wanted to move there. It was infested with crack dealers, but most of them were more scared of me and my mates than I was of them. I knew the estate well and knew some good people lived there.

Before I met S.B.I had been seeing a man who lived in what they laughingly called the posh bit (a bit of the canal and a couple of trees), but he was a student and had gone back to Hong Kong. At the same time I was seeing a man from Saint Kitts – my Mum said (something like) my love life always resembled the United Nations. Anyway, I knew S.B. (who was still a postman) used to make excuses like how he could not work out the numbers on the Marquess. He would stick the letters back in the nearest postbox. To be fair, it was a brave postman who actually delivered on this notorious estate and S.B. wasn't that brave.

I thought to myself I might not get any letters, but if he finds me at all, the Old Bill will find him first. As a rule, the giros were distributed amongst the needles and dog-shit at the bottom of the stairs by (usually two) postmen, accompanied by a policeman and one of the estate's very own security guards. Although they thought I was deranged, asking to be housed there, the council went for it (it gave them a measure of how desperate I was).

It took three months, but when I moved in I was happier than a dog with two dicks! S.B.'s state of mind may have scared me, but crack dealers didn't – although I found out later it was not that simple. But life never is, is it? For the moment I was happy, and felt safe away from S.B. and his threats.

I bought a bicycle and cycled along the canal and on the pavement via Essex Road to work in Kentish Town. No-one but a suicidal nut-case would try and dodge the traffic on a bike.

Actually, much later in life it was on Essex Road that Marc, my husband now (not that I intend having any more husbands) came home in a state of shock one time, after seeing someone come off a motorbike. When he heard his neck crack, he knew he was dead. They knew it was dangerous, so the Old Bill let you cycle on the pavement without giving you too much grief.

Gradually, as one of my work colleagues had said would happen, S.B. realised he was powerless to bully me any more! Rather than aggravate the situation I decided I had no reason to divorce him at this time (I had tried once, but was intimidated by his threats to kill me and himself). I thought to myself, if I ever did want to marry again (which seemed unlikely at the time) I would sort it out then. In fact his Mum gave him the money for a quickie divorce a long time later. When I thought he had accepted the split, I went back to see him at the flat, in order to extract my remaining possessions. He would only agree if I met him alone, so I took a large knife just in case, but I did not need it – he was almost civil and agreed to give me some money for the wardrobe I had left behind. I think he just did not want anyone else to know how badly he had treated me when people knew how much I had adored him.

Mike's band were going to play in Oregon. At the same time my Mum and Dad gave me some money. I said to my Dad – I could piss it up against the wall, save it, or go to

America with a rock band. He said something like, "Of course, it's your money after all – have you packed?!"

The adage that travel broadens the mind is spot on! My preconceptions of America were many – some were accurate, but most of them were rubbish. As Oscar Wilde (and later George Bernard Shaw) said, "We are two nations divided by a common language!" – until you go, you don't realise how culturally different we really are.

Before we went to Oregon to meet up with the band, three of us flew to Reno, as Mike wanted to do some gambling. The bass guitarist and I been occasional lovers for quite a while, and he had helped me move from S.B.'s flat. I thought this was really cool. Not that I was suddenly going to stop being the band groupie or anything (I had already notched up two other band members who were there in America, not to mention the countless other members of Mike's band over the years) – but I did especially like him. Needless to say, he and I spent more time shagging than we did gambling. I was well up for it and so was he. Unfortunately (Mike assured me) as soon as we got to Oregon, he had prearranged to meet a large lady he was involved with, and he did have a reputation for being fond of the larger lady. Mike might like to extol voyeurism, but of course we all enjoy a bit of voyeurism – otherwise we would not like dirty films (although if I ever see that one Mike had of the virgins being shagged over motorbikes in a church again, I will scream!). I think he disliked being a wall flower while all this sex was going on in the same room.

In Reno, we all won at something at first (it's rumoured everyone wins the first time to encourage you to gamble). I was not a great gambler so I did a lot of sitting at the bar (when I wasn't otherwise engaged). It was cool being in 'Sin City', and I liked the naughtiness. There were lots of Mexicans in Reno, and all the Americans loved our accents. Mike had an American friend called Steve, who gambled the most enormous amounts of money, so the staff gave him loads of attention. He was also completely reckless hedonist I'm pleased to say (like the rest of us). He flew over to see the first few gigs when we joined the band in Oregon. At one point he and Mike were driving along a narrow one way flyover, next to each other, passing a bottle of whiskey back and forth through the window (they knew the police could not catch them at the speed they were doing). He also enjoyed going at ludicrous speed with too many passengers around very thin and windy mountain roads, with a hundred foot drop the other side. I admit I was enjoying the danger, and I was not concerned for my safety due to being completely wrecked on a cocktail of illegal drugs. This may have added to the excitement!

They did a lot of gigs in Washington State (and lots of other places – we went to Salt Lake City but it was closed and had been for a while by the look of it). We hit at least five states in the U.S. and the thing that I noticed most was the racial segregation. Everywhere we went had a black area, where some brave white people lived and a white area where only well-to-do black people seemed to reside. This alone would stop me moving to the U.S. without a very good reason! On the bright side, I did get to see the killer whales in Depot Bay, even if it was from a distance. That was mega-exciting!

When we went to Seattle, Mike introduced me to Courtney Love, but I was a bit underwhelmed. She seemed to spend much of her time being rude to people like a spoiled brat. I did however meet a sweet lady called Maggie who had a lovely daughter called Bridget. Bridget told me all about her Irish lineage, of which she was very proud. I watched Mike and Maggie fall in love, which was a really cool thing to witness. She had a stunning singing voice, and she and her friends seemed to go between New Orleans and the beautiful Cannon Beach singing – what a splendid way to live!

When I got back from Oregon, most evenings I would go and see a particular band I liked, or lurk around in the Hare and Hounds (S.B. never went near the place). This madhouse was a great music venue. Chas and Dave practically lived there and lots of famous musicians wobbled about the place. Mike Khan played there a lot. The Balham Alligators often played and me, Robin

McKidd's missus Philippa, and Annie Gunn used to prop up the bar – and my mate Luddy Samms of Drifters fame would be about jamming or doing Mike's brother's unique karaoke (Timmy used sing 'Stairway to Heaven' stunningly). Luddy and I used to sing 'Summertime' together – he would sing the Ella Fitzgerald bit and I the Louis Armstrong bit. Louis Armstrong is my best (and only) impression. Joe Hale (the oldest pub guv'nor in London, still working at 84) would be behind the bar and sometimes his wife Marie (79) would sing (usually 'Dear Mister Gable' or 'Crazy'), or would sit on the floor and put both feet behind her ears (showing all her drawers in the process of course). Joe and Marie had been in showbiz for more years than most people live, and publicans for over thirty. They had worked with Gracie Fields at the Old Collins Music Hall. Apart from singing and whistling Marie had done all sorts of stuff in the Music Hall and Joe Hale had his famous big band. They had worked with Marie Lloyd and told hundreds of stories about what they got up to in the old days and neither of them had been saints, that's for sure.

Joe tried to console me (about S.B.) by pointing out that he'd fetched Marie a wallop before now. I couldn't help thinking that it was likely she hit him first, or at least hardest (I had seen them fight). Joe was still managing Hughie Green who he couldn't stand (and that makes at least three of us including my Dad). When I asked why he managed someone he couldn't stand he would say his favourite phrase – "Don't be so foolhardy!"

Money, as far as he was concerned, was the only reason you would do any work. Marie and her mate ('Jim and Lemonade' – I never heard him say lemonade and he never drunk doubles... bottles maybe, but not doubles – God knows what his real name was) would sit for hours, pissed out of their noses. The game was for one of them to find an old song the other couldn't sing in tune and remember all the words to. There did not appear to be such a song. Their repertoire was astonishing. Upstairs in their flat (yes, it also was bedlam), you would normally find their blind Doberman or three legged cat, or their other treasure – the drunken cleaner sleeping it off. There was also occasionally their mate from Clacton, where they had a seaside home, changing into the most unconvincing woman you have ever seen. When he came downstairs in drag, no one took a blind bit of notice, although he did get more drinks in the make-up. I still miss Joe and Marie – I can hear him now in his broad Scots yelling – "Come on now you lucky people! You'll all miss the blue movie!"

So having drawn a line under the traumatic split with S.B. that had nearly cost me my sanity, I flew out of the frying pan into the fire. I met a charming and handsome man from Merseyside. He had a sort of almost swarthy quality, like Eric Burdon – irresistible. We met in the pub next to the Jobcentre. He was much brighter than S.B.

and, unfortunately for me, a much better liar. He was working on the building site nearby, but I realised quite quickly most of his income was criminal. Most of it seemed to be from credit cards bearing someone else's name, by the time I had realised the extent of this, I had fallen for him hook, line, and sinker. I took a break from work, to sort my head out after S.B. (they owed me three months' holiday so I took this and a bit more in lieu), most of which I spent with John, often in his Dad's house in Wallasey, and staying with him in other parts of Merseyside. I adored it there, and people were friendly (even if they would rob you while you were not looking).

He showed me Alan Bleasdale's house in New Brighton. I also got chatted up in the Dale Inn by a sweet man called Jan Molby. I had no idea he was a famous footballer until John tried to get me to go home with him, so the rest of them could rob him, or some such cobblers. I was not sure how seriously to take this, but extricated myself from the situation by pointing out that footballers have minders who are likely to hurt anyone trying to interfere with their precious charge. John was full of shit like that. Stupidly (and naïvely) I took him to Mike's place and he robbed it later. Mike put a knife to my throat, ostensibly to see if I was in on it (he was pissed at the time). I just laughed at him and pointed out that I was as likely to rob him as he was cut me with a knife. Not only was I not perturbed, but I gave him loads of shit before he removed the knife. I pointed out that naïve I may be, but treacherous I wasn't.

I knew John wasn't daft, but I was usually one step ahead, and that theft was the one exception – I just never thought he would sink so low as to rob my best mate. When I was finally convinced of his guilt, I thought I would never forgive myself for being so stupid.

Before this John and I enjoyed Wallasey and I do not regret the time I spent there, especially with his family. It was the only place I went where they did more singing than Wales, and they were all brilliant. They would all squash into the 'back kitchen', fill themselves full of the most enormous amounts of liquid refreshment and sing like Dusty Springfield.

I enjoyed meeting his cousin (who was as much of a 'scally' as John was), and his Auntie who was very knowledgeable about Liverpool's slave trade (being of mixed lineage and her family coming from those roots). She was proper Liverpool, not a 'woolyback', and read my tarot cards.

After a while I got fed up with John and his mates poncing off me, and next time he fucked off I changed the locks. He decided to reappear one day. Of course him being an experienced burglar he thought he would climb in the window. Being pissed at the time and it being three floors up, he broke his leg. He made all sorts of promises but although I was always one step ahead of him, which pissed him off, I found myself stupidly following him around like a lost puppy, catching him flagrantly (or bang to rights) with other women and then trying to believe the excuses (it was a bit like being Rene's missus in 'Allo Allo' – and I was indeed being a 'stupid woman'). In the end, after I had caught up with him on The Isle of Wight he buggered off and left me. I was heartbroken at the time – suicidal in fact (for at least an hour). My friend Che had predicted the end of this torrid romance in the tarot cards, but I did not really need them to tell me what I had already known for a long time. After a while I stopped feeling sorry for myself and got on with it. Life was too short for another nervous breakdown, I said to myself. By the time I found out about the robbery, he was long gone, and that just made me think good riddance.

Generally, I had tried to avoid hooking up with my customers or colleagues at the Jobcentre, as apart from not being very professional it was complicated. I did not fancy many of them anyway. I had already caused a big rumour with one of my managers who let me stay over a couple of times, when we had all been drinking in Camden and I had no way of getting back to Teddington – and there was enough ol' chat when I disappeared with an adviser, after office drinkies, from time to time. God knows why that was gossip – the Civil Service was one of the most insular places I knew. They all seem to marry someone from the office and if they've got a bit on the side, they are from the same bloody office – what the fuck do they talk about at home?

Anyway, I was flattered when this very young lad (not jailbait but much younger than me) gave me a load of old chat when I was interviewing him. By the time he had caught up with me in the Hare and Hounds he'd got a job and was off my books, so I thought why not? He was all rippling muscles and his dark black skin shined, even when he was not sweating. Why wouldn't you? Despite the mutual lust we drifted apart. I suppose the age difference was more significant than I thought. Anyway I didn't want another live in partner at this point. I was beginning to value my independence.

Back on the Marquess, I befriended a woman who Sam (my boss from Clapton Youth Centre) had been trying to help. She had moved into a downstairs flat and reckoned she was being targeted because of her colour (I doubted the oiks on the estate would have guessed her lineage). Sam had suggested she seek my protection as a sympathetic ear, although even I thought she was laying it on a bit thick with the victim of racism/sexism stuff. Even her South American accent was a bit of a stretch, and in terms of victimisation, and she was lighter skinned that most people I knew who considered themselves white, but I tried not to make a judgement. After all, what do I know about it? I knew there was no logic to be found in any racist attitude, so I supported her as much as I could and she got herself to move out pretty quickly to somewhere safer.

Then there were twins in their fifties, whose family were reputed to be the local yardies on the Estate. I knew they were naughty boys but their lineage generated a certain amount of fear among the idiots. They were of African descent from the Caribbean and albinistic (people with white skin and red eyes). I used to have a drink with them and their families at the 'Percy' – The Perseverance, a pub on the edge of the estate full of naughty people. I found them charming, but then, I had the sense not to ask them what they did for a living (especially as they knew what I did). I rarely went in the estate pub (there was no point unless you wanted to buy nicked gear), which was full of daft kids who wanted to cause mayhem so they could show how hard they were, so I had no use for it, but a friend went in there and overheard a bunch of tossers discussing who on the estate was worth burgling, and my name came up. Apparently I wasn't a good idea as I knew 'that Mike Khan' and he knew some serious faces.

Despite my hedonistic behaviour and my reputation as a hell-raiser I began to enjoy the flair I had for my little job, and stopped looking at it as a stop-gap. I found I had a good connection with people and used my persuasive skills and my acting acumen to persuade people that they wanted a job and that they could do the job that they wanted. Although I did a couple of commercials I had grown weary of the constant uphill struggle that acting requires and decided to work on being good at the day job for a while. I was very happy in my little place. Until I moved to my present house in Norfolk it was the place I had felt most comfortable in and by far the nicest flat I had lived in so far. However I kept having a recurring dream of a man standing outside my bedroom window (he would have to be floating three storeys or about 30 feet above the ground) pointing a shotgun into the flat. Perhaps those of you who don't believe in premonition will explain this to me after reading the next couple of chapters!

CHAPTER TEN
Pork, Sausage and Mash

One night it was a bit boring in the Hare and Hounds, so I stayed for about half an hour after work and then thought, "Where shall I go?"

At this time I had not been in the King's Head for about five years. I walked in and threw my carpet bag on the floor, and started to go upstairs to the loo. Sitting at the bar (almost on his own) was a hunky ginger fella with an African bottom – amongst other things. Other people even in cosmopolitan London had trouble, but I spotted his lineage straight away, despite the freckles. He warned me not to leave my bag there in case it gets nicked – I threw a remark over my shoulder about having nothing worth stealing. We got chatting and the drinks were flowing. As the pub filled up I could see the confusion on his face. I guessed he was thinking something like, "I've never met this woman before but everybody knows her really well – all the bar staff, the local bank robbers, the local drug dealer, even the geezer from the Maltese cafe next door..." – and plenty more besides!

Eventually (it was obvious I'd pulled), I said, "It's a bit boring in here, I'm going back to my local – the Hare and

Hounds. We could go there for a drink and then we could go back to my flat and have sex if you like!"

He did like and since there were no discernible protests we did just that. He tells everyone he held out for at least two halves of lager as he's not cheap. After a day or so of spending quite a bit of time together, he turned up with a suitcase. I thought "Oh bloody hell, not again!"

It wasn't the lack of subtlety, I quite liked that. It was just that I was only just over being hurt by John and it was still raw. But I liked him a lot, and after all the sex was good, so I thought we'll see where life takes us. So it wasn't love at first sight or any of that romantic nonsense. In the early days as a pair of like-minded hedonists, we spent most of the time together off our tits. Mick the Gorilla and I had remained good mates, and he and Marc took to each other straight away (they had a lot in common).

There was a cool music pub just by the estate called Disgraceland. The three of us turned up looking as though we owned the place, and the patrons were a little taken aback by three such scary looking people – I don't know if they thought we were coppers or our reputation preceded us. Among the racket we made in praise of the band, Mick was banging on the table and shouting in broad 'Beffnal Green' "Yus mate!"

By the end of the gig the whole audience were on their feet and shouting "Yus mate!" at the end of each song! I don't know if that was because they were terrified of us three, or they just liked the band. When we went back the next time we were treated like royalty and written on the dart board in chalk were the immortal words 'Yus mate'!

One day I was walking up Camden High Street at lunchtime with a baby-faced lad, dubbed 'The Boy'. We were, as usual, running the gauntlet of beggars. By the Tube, by the cashpoints etc. – but one made the mistake of picking on me (presumably because I was heavily pregnant at the time). He kept standing in front of me threateningly, but after a few choice words, I violently thrust him aside. He lost his balance and collapsed drunkenly over a parked car. I mention this story as it was when The Boy recounted it to Marc in the pub that he began to get the measure of me, and realise I was not some daft girl looking for a man to protect me.

I did not expect to get pregnant as some stupid doctor had told me that S.B. and I could not have children. I thought it was me that could not have children. Assuming this was the case I had contemplated adopting a traveller's orphan when I was in Dublin, but after a little research I found out she was not an orphan and it was some kind of scam by her family. The doctor had not had the good grace to point out, or even indicate, that S.B. was firing blanks as he drank too much (perhaps there is a God of some sort after all). So when I had discovered I was pregnant, it was quite a shock to Marc and I, but we took to parenthood well.

While I was still in the early stages, I got this terrible bout of flu and was laid up for about five weeks with a fever. When I got better, I had this daft idea that my baby was no longer kicking and therefore was dead. There was all sorts of reasons for this ridiculous piece of paranoia (some historic that I don't wish to talk about), but a lot of it was to do with having been convinced I could not bear children in the first place. When I started getting pain, Marc called the ambulance straight away. Despite being told it was only 'Braxton Hicks', it took the ambulance some time to get into the estate. Marc found them on the wrong side and directed them to the flat. They carried me down the stairs and then one of the paramedics recognised me, so all the way up a completely clogged Holloway Road he distracted me with chat about all the extraordinary people we knew, from various madhouse watering holes in North London, interspersed with my loud and anguished screams. They took me almost straight to the delivery room, gave me an epidural (on my insistence) and the room filled with people of all different races (even I noticed), in all different uniforms, while I started to give birth. It reminded me of the United Colors of Benetton commercial on telly at the time.

I was warned my baby was in distress and I may lose it (I had only just been convinced she was still alive). In Islington they do not tell you the sex of the baby until it is born for all sorts of reasons. One of the midwives went off duty and an Irish lady came in her place. When she came close enough to me, I asserted that my baby was going to be a girl. The name on her badge was Roisin – the girl's name we had chosen! It was only then, at that moment, in the clamour of a room full of excited doctors and one terrified mum, that I was able to convince myself that she was going to be fine. Then like some dreadful Ozzie comedy sketch the doctor in charge put a sucker thing on the baby's head (ventouse), put one foot on up on the end of the bed and pulled!

When I saw my beautiful girl, I burst into tears, but I suppose I'm not the first mum to do that! I realised not only was she alive but beautiful! When Marc and my mum and dad came to visit I kept pulling her in and out of the small hole in the side of the incubator to cuddle her (and they knew how clumsy I was), saying, "Ooops mind your 'ead!" as I nearly bumped it on the plastic. This sent them into fits of giggles.

When I came to have Rory, they had decided to induce him. Despite being a lot less hysterical than with Roisin, and my warnings about being a wimp with pain, I screamed the hospital down like a demented banshee, before they stopped making excuses and gave me the drugs I had been demanding like a desperate junkie! By the time I had had an epidural, I told the remaining midwife (there had never more than two this time) about Roisin and the midwife of the same name. So when he was born, she shouted in her broad accent "It's a Rory!"

They were frantically busy so she asked if I would be OK on my own, pressed an alarm in my hand and sprinted off at the double, leaving me cuddling my beautiful baby. Despite the tears rolling down my cheeks, I could hear how busy it was, as I could hear one after another baby being born – first the woman screaming (usually at the father it would seem), then that distinctive baby cry. I was a little taken aback when my dad (an ardent supporter of women's lib) was so excited by having a boy grandchild. It never occurred to me that the boy child thing would impress him (my sister has two gorgeous girls), not that I thought for a moment that he and my Mum made any distinction, in any way, between their four gorgeous grandchildren.

Life was quite hard with two sprogs (and a big lolloping hound) in such a tiny one-bedroom flat, on a rough estate, but life overtakes you sometimes and you just get on with it and count your blessings. I had obviously got a reasonably steady job, but we could ill afford childcare, and it was a nightmare trying to find anyone you could trust. So Marc took care of Roisin while I was at work, for about a year. We had Rory quite soon after Roisin, and by this time I was forty and we did not expect to have anywhere better to live (although we were going to have a bloody good try).

I put in for a bigger flat, but I was not holding my breath. Marc decided he wanted a bit of adult company during the day. In the end we found a great child-minder on the estate, and he went to work. He did a variety of jobs bouncing in the Paradise Club at night, but he was much safer in the hardcore gay place upstairs (a dangerous looney bin full of serious blinged up and tooled up 'yardies'), and did courier work in the day. Both were seriously dangerous jobs, especially the Paradise – I nearly got lynched in there one night when I was wobbling around pissed. I watched Marc take this huge knife off a complete psychopath, and decided not to go back there and keep myself awake at night worrying about his safety.

One of Marc's old uni mates had a party in Stoke Newington. His girlfriend invited Marc's mad ex. We had a great time, but she and her friend managed to make themselves as popular as a turd in a swimming pool. They seemed to upset people they had only just met. I got stuck in the loo with her and her nasty friend. I was seven months pregnant with Roisin. They were trying lamely to take the piss in that really cowardly, nasty way, as if they weren't quite meaning me to hear, although it was perfectly obvious their inane banter was not directed at anyone else. Hitting anyone is not my style (especially as any problem with the Old Bill would have lost me my job). So I got hold of the ex's wrists and held her so she could not move. She was visibly shocked by my strength and I was confident that neither me nor my baby were going to get hurt.

The other twat was behind me so I pre-empted a punch in the kidneys and got ready to move. Instead she ran out screaming, obviously hoping to be rescued by some random man, a species they had earlier professed to hate so much. At that time a woman I vaguely recognised came in ostensibly to use the loo, although it was obvious she'd been sent in (she was bigger than me). She said, "There is no need for that!"

Undeterred, I calmly continued trying to talk sense with the nitwit, suggesting that she should stop harassing us and pay back the money she owed Marc's mum, whilst still holding her wrists tightly in case she fetched me a wallop. The presence of the other woman prompted her foolishly to pretend to be brave, and she uttered something childish like "Why should I?"

I replied, "Because she is a pensioner who apparently got you out of trouble, and because I don't like to see her ripped off!"

The other lady came out the loo and while washing her hands said to me, "I've changed my mind – carry on!"

By this time Miss Witless was scared shitless and visibly shaken, but was obviously not bright enough to understand reason, so I gave up and let go. She ran off promptly without giving me any more grief. We bumped into this idiot in the Hawley Arms, after Roisin was born.

We were having lunch and Roisin was getting a lot of attention, particularly from a big bunch of large dangerous black fellas Marc knew from the market. She was with her South American 'boyfriend'. I'll explain – the Islington gay mafia (of which we were sort of honorary members) remonstrated one by one that there was no way he liked women or would even sleep with women – not even for money. The information they would not part with is why every gay fella we spoke to hated him with a vengeance, but would not explain why! I'll let you hazard a few guesses!

Anyway he (just as daft as her) started throwing unfounded accusations across the room, a struggle for him in his broken English. I was worried the market lads were going to become violent, but instead they had the situation well in hand and took the piss mercilessly until they buggered off, with their tails between their legs. The third encounter with this twat was when she tried to recount a story to convince me Marc was violent (I think this was the closest she got to being nice). Roisin screamed as soon she came near her (good judge of character, our Roisin). The dozy twat told me three different versions of a story about Marc breaking her arm. Even her mate (who was supposed to be a trainee solicitor, but you knew she hadn't got the 'ackers') did not believe her and suddenly and conveniently remembered she had to be somewhere else.

After this she gave up and left us alone and June, Marc's mum, eventually wrote off the debt.

Roisin was very cute – so cute we were once asked by a PR man in the King's Head if we wanted to put her in films, but an actress who we were chatting to at the time who was working with French and Saunders advised us not to as she did not feel it was good for the child.

Anyway, we were in an Irish pub called the Albion, with Roisin. The customers liked her name (although Irish names are not unusual, especially in London). It is traditional to put a coin in a newborn baby's hand, for luck. It was our first day off together and as we were with some friends who were driving and said they would keep an eye on her if we wanted to have a drink, we ended up getting legless. She certainly earned her keep that day!

I was beginning to realise Marc was not being sexist when he said some of his exes were murder in an empty house. I almost encountered another one. I was very pregnant with Roisin and sitting waiting for Marc in the King's Head chatting to my mate 'Puddly' Dave (from scouse-land for those not familiar with the vernacular). Two seats up was a woman who kept gawping at me, so obviously Dave looked back at her and said "What?"

He asked me, teasingly, if I knew who the father was. I said, "You cheeky bugger, you know the father's Marc!"

At that point the staring woman threw an obvious hissy fit (all on her own and by herself) and stormed out. I very quickly caught on. Marc walked in later, but before Dave (or I) could mention it he'd rushed off to get some fags from the shop. Apparently while walking down Upper Street, 'some child' as he put it stopped him and demanded he got in the old wreck he was driving. Marc just said "Don't be silly!" and went to walk on, then he realised this Jane (the one who had stormed out the King's Head, unbeknown to him) was in the back seat, so he asked her what was going on.

She said after they had shagged each other (and then she'd blanked him), some jewellery had gone missing (if there was any jewellery in the first place – Marc pointed out the most likely thief there was an idiot called Skilly. I knew Skilly as well, he was banned from my flat, and he was the first one I thought of as well).

Later on in the King's Head, one of her mates (Robin) chucked the same accusation at Marc. As I told her to sling her hook, she opened her mouth to say something and Puddly Dave shook his head violently to tell her to back off. I should explain I had something of a reputation that preceded me, having been resident bouncer. In case anyone showed any suspicion that they thought it wasn't warranted, I had a couple of little party tricks, like picking up Britannia tables by one leg with one hand, turning them over and plonking them on the tatty old theatre seats that lined the bar. Or picking up a seven foot basketball player, fireman's lift style, and removing him from the premises.

'O', our nickname here for the gentleman in question, enjoyed playing along with this. Any show of strength by a woman frightened the hell out of stroppy hangers-on at closing time.

Robin took Dave's advice. Later on, presumably this Jane had given up this crap. It would seem to have been born of some sort of strange but ill thought out bid to get back with Marc.

We did not see her again, but Robin turned up at a rough music pub called Molly Malones' when Mike's band was playing. I had Roisin in a sling so I went to find Marc, in case there was any trouble. When I found him Robin was already there apologising for believing Jane's nonsense.

It was an interesting gig at Molly's, as on the same night some 'nutter' drove a chopper into the bar, and apologised because he did not know the baby was in the bar (I was able to take her outside frequently in the hot summer anyway because of the smoke). This was a repeat of an earlier performance by a mate called Carol, who drove her bike into the King's Head after a rendition of Mike Khan's 'Motorbike Lady', which had been written about her. Both kids were used to going to the pub for a little while, and as long as they remained entertained by it all, it broadened their horizons (and ours), which is probably why they were so well behaved in pubs.

At another one of Mike's gigs, Luddy Samms did some singing. Some dozy man was all over him like the suit he was wearing, that fitted where it touched (Luddy was already a veteran of the music business, having sung with bands like the Drifters), and was trying to convince Luddy that he was the bloke to make him famous. Marc and I had a quiet word.

Roisin and Rory are very different. Roisin was always the tough one who protected her brother, and he was younger and a little sensitive. Later at school a big kid who was a bully hit Rory, who ran away crying. Rory was much bigger than Roisin by then – she was tiny – but it did not stop her giving this big bully a punch in the belly and warning him to keep away from her brother. He wasn't arguing. The teachers found it hard to chastise her under the circumstances and so did I. Rory may have been a little timid with other kids then, but he was noisier and good at bashing things and breaking toys, or in the popular London/Caribbean parlance, 'him mash it up'! My mum's lovely friend Mary Crewe used to call me Sausage, and I nicknamed Roisin the same. So our children were often called Sausage and Mash.

Marc and I decided to get married, mainly for the kids. I don't mean that we weren't happy together, just that kids tend to feel more secure if their parents have got a daft bit of paper making it legal. We had an extraordinary wedding – the King's Head was not available so we picked a nice little pub called the Empress of Prussia. We had lots of nice guests and the wedding presents were fantastic, including things talented people brought like a painting they had done for the occasion, or a hat for me to wear, designed and made themselves. My mum and dad and June and Philip, Marc's parents, got on like a house on fire. Dad and Philip were both film buffs although Philip was an Oxford Don, my Dad also lectured in colleges, and sadly never finished his book on Hollywood Art Directors. Although June was a named artist, my Mum had been designing dresses and doing watercolours for years, so they had a lot in common. I understand they all ended up rat-arsed! Apart from me having to threaten a couple of gatecrashing junkies, things went really well!

Until June died, my Mum always sent her a birthday prezzy (something June was not brilliant at remembering herself, by her own admission), and I know she was touched by this as she told me. I was not sure about Marc's mum and dad at first. His mum seemed to equate me with his last girlfriend, assuming I was not only just like her, but that we were bessie-mates – neither of these things were the case. I did not have the dubious pleasure of meeting the ex until later.

Later on June and Philip changed their minds and we became very close. I used to go with Philip to the local market where his mate would get us to try sorts of cheeses, that were so ripe they wore trainers to make a quick getaway (June and Marc labelled us both culinary perverts). June showed me her paintings and talked about her life and books, and read my tarot cards (I had been reading for quite some time). She told me about how she got her women's poetry book published. She had approached this publisher who tried to brush her off. After some persistence by June, he handed her an invitation to his wedding in Sri Lanka, where he promised to discuss the book. It was obvious that he assumed this black woman from the arse-end of Liverpool was unlikely to be able to afford the trip. Although, technically, that was probably true at the time, June painted a picture for a competition (something to do with the Guru Sri-Rajneesh) of a mixed race couple canoodling on the back of an elephant. She won the competition (and £1,000), and turned up to the wedding, where he felt obliged to publish her book.

I felt sort of uncomfortable when June called Marc his nickname 'Piggy'. It seemed at odds with what she was trying to achieve at the time. Marc had been a fat kid with glasses (reminiscent of the character of 'Lord of the Flies'), who got teased. I looked upon it like black people calling each other the 'N-word'. In the end she persuaded me I was being precious, and it was true he did like the name. Piggy was her personal nickname, but I have to admit Roisin, Rory and I call him Porkie or Porks now. So I admit, she was right and I was being a little P.C. about the whole thing. She was a complicated but remarkable woman and I miss her and Philip now. Even though I did not know them for long I often think about them.

It did not seem very long after that that I lost my Dad, certainly the most devastating thing that has happened in my life. I don't want to go on about how much I miss him, although I do, because you did not know him. We had a lovely little funeral (planned by him) attended just the close family, in addition to some apt words, and music of his era alongside badly recorded (by me) excerpts from classical music he liked. I neither appreciate, nor particularly understand Mozart or whoever the other geezer was – sorry Dad. I had however assumed the rest of the family were not such philistines, but after the first one went on, and on... infernally, my sister put a stop to the second one, to everyone's obvious relief (they were trying to be polite as well) and slight amusement! I don't believe in the religious idea of someone watching over you, but if my Dad had been able to see us at the time, he would have been having a little giggle to himself at his last laugh!

Sometimes in life, even today, a little sarcastic voice comes into my head, that sounds a lot like his, and tells me I know the answer to something. "It's obvious!" he's saying – thanks Dad!

Chapter 11
Murder!

One evening I had fallen asleep watching the telly. 'Mr Nosy' was looking out the window. "Here, come and look at this!" he said. I could hear the usual anarchy and mayhem outside, but the noise level in the evening was always high. There was the usual cacophony, including four different sources of deafening music (none particularly to my taste). After all, the walls were thin enough to hear your next door neighbour having a piss. Or, as in our next door neighbour's case, shifting nicked gear up the stairs at four in the morning.

When Marc was taking our dog Murphy out for a walk around the estate at about six in the morning (that is, a walk around the needles on the handkerchief of green the other side of the estate), and two big fellas were taking turns at kicking the front door in, he didn't necessarily think they were coppers. "What the fuck are you doing?" he asked politely.

They just told him to shut up, so, still thinking they may be criminals, but guessing they were Babylon, he said, "Either you tell me what's going on or I'll let this dog off the lead!"

By this time Murphy was giving it large!

"We're the police!" said one of them, flashing a badge.

"Well why the hell didn't you say so?" Marc said more quietly. While calming down the dog he saw the geezer hiding the other side of our front door, with a rifle and a jacket marked 'Police', and thought it might be politic to walk the dog later, in case it all kicked off.

This sort of thing was not unusual. We had already witnessed police and security guards chasing some bloke across the rooftops who was sporting a Kalashnikov (they were all the rage on the estate).

Anyway, back to that one night and the insistence that I 'come and have a look'. I was weary of the nightly circus, and knowing that this was the time for all the animals to come out to play, I cavalierly remarked, "I'm not interested, I've seen it all before!"

Then after a while, it suddenly occurred to me how quiet Marc and the rabble had become. Little did I know of the events unfolding outside my window, as I ironically watched 'The Bill', and when Marc came away from the window he was as white as a sheet. He was visibly in shock. This prompted me to go and see what all the fuss was about. What I only caught the tail end of was a huge gang of teenagers stabbing a bloke that lived only a few doors down from me – thirty-two times. My babysitter's husband (nicknamed 'Builder's Bum') had held him in his arms while he 'died' twice and the ambulance tried to get into the centre of the estate (not realising it had been blocked off to discourage joyriders).

For quite some time, in fact, there was more of him on the pavement than being cherished by Builder's Bum while the life was being sucked out of him. He was dead before they took him away. Even when the flowers started arriving, a big pool of claret marked the place where he had been murdered. Some of those who brought flowers had been standing there while he was murdered.

Builder's Bum was never the same person again and when we saw him in court, both he and my child-minder looked gaunt and ill and walked around like two people who had seen a ghost. In a sense that was what they had seen.

Marc had already had one altercation with a couple of the murderers, over a stolen works van. He had managed to stop himself being stabbed while one of the gang leaders slashed at him with a knife – it just caught the end of his nose. It seems that they took exception to him enquiring about the works van, as indeed it was them who had stolen it (to hide a nicked motorbike apparently). When he called the police about this unprovoked attack they were not interested. They would be interested now!

By the time I really registered what was going on and looked out the window myself, the pack of baying wolves had begun clearing. Eventually the Old Bill turned up, looking lost as usual, and were running round the estate trying to round up the perpetrators like chickens with their heads cut off. It was complete pandemonium! The police later in the press insisted the murder was not racist, but part of an on-going war with the nearby Packington Estate, but none of the people I saw hanging around were from outside the Marquess, and the perpetrators certainly lived on the estate. In any case, the Packington Estate had as many people of colour and as much racism as the Marquess.

Sensibly, most of the estate has been pulled down now, in the hope that this kind racially motivated gang warfare won't happen again. Of course it has, often and recently. Efforts by the community to control this kind of mess are always thwarted by the circumstances. These only come about where at least three thousand people (officially – in reality you could treble that figure), some of whom already had enormous social problems, have been squashed into a space just shy of 500 metres square.

After the murder, we found out a few things on the grapevine – firstly there was a rumour that this same bunch had killed a tramp at the front of the estate but, because he had no family, the police dropped the case. Also, Marc went up in the lift at the court with their first victim. He was of mixed lineage and they threw a pot of yoghurt over him and shouted "This will make you white!" and then threw him over the fence, out of the way (the main drug squabble was not with him, but his cousin, who they murdered).

Careful not to reveal he knew who he was, or to discuss the trial, Marc asked him if he had a cold (he kept sniffing). He explained to Marc that he was a Charlie addict (cocaine – probably crack). He was fourteen.

The complete anarchy on the estate came as a surprise to the police. They never came on the estate, unless they were mob handed and in a vehicle, to arrest someone really serious (like a drugs baron). If there was a community copper, I had never met one. Young people were shocked when they discovered they could no longer walk around the estate, looking menacing, brandishing bits of wood and baseball bats, without being arrested or told off. I did not think I suffered fools gladly, but it's amazing how much you tolerate in this sort of environment without noticing your very soul is being affected by a constant onslaught of unnecessary violent behaviour. They seemed to regard curbing their attitudinal stance an impingement of their human right (...to be a dickhead).

The next few days were a bit of a blur, so my memory is hazy. Police were running in and out of the flat while several of the gang looked up at the window, pointed at the children and drew their finger across their throat. They had already told us verbally, before the police came round, that they would kill the children if we testified. In fact, had they not been afraid of Murphy (who was a pretty scary and large dog, bought off some miscreant in South London).

I knew they would have killed my children without a second thought. I knew we had to get out, before we were all killed. The police wired us up in case of an emergency, and muttered something about moving us to Camden. I knew that was not going to happen, and anyway I did not trust the police to put our safety first. They seemed much more interested in Marc's testimony. Marc was by far their only credible witness. Most of the others were crack dealers, part of the prevalent gangs – yes, there was more than one even on the estate – or had already had a complete mental breakdown.

So Marc was by far the sanest person who saw the murder, although it was some months before he stopped waking up in the middle of the night screaming and shaking. I was very much a London girl and knew I would miss the place I'd lived in for over forty years (and I still do), but we packed what belongings we had in the car (and yes, amusingly enough we still had the bank robber's beamer) – and got the fuck out of there!

So we all descended on my poor sister, like a rash. Needless to say, she and Patrick looked after us much better than the police did. To extricate ourselves from the situation, we had to take ourselves to Norfolk straight away, which riled the police, but we were not going to hang around while they dithered. It was our lives at stake. I also had to jump up and down at the Jobcentre until they gave me a transfer as well. They offered me a job in Downham Market – a place so remote I still have not been there – and the police offered to re house us somewhere equally obscure (I forget where).

Knowing Norfolk well, I explained that everyone would want to know why Londoners suddenly arrived in the middle of nowhere with two young sprogs. Anyway, how would a non-driver get to work? They had no idea how awful the transport system in Norfolk was (and still is). Eventually, my District Manager, who had a good head on his shoulders (and a good heart), pulled rank and forced through a transfer to Great Yarmouth Jobcentre (just about doable). So one day I was working in Camden, getting people jobs such as 'Race Equality Enabler', and three days later (yes – two whole days special leave), I was working in Yarmouth, trying to work out what a share fisherman or chicken catcher did. It was quite a culture shock for me, even though I'd lived all over the shop. I pointed out to the police (who were still miffed) that we had fled to my sister's for our own safety, thus saving them the job of looking after the witnesses to *our* murder.

I had forgotten how quiet Norfolk was. My sister's is right out in the countryside, and not only was it pitch black outside at night (no street-lights), but the silence was deafening. Although I couldn't sleep (that is not unusual), I started to calm down and the panic inside that was making me shake was beginning to subside. I had managed to ensconce myself in Yarmouth Jobcentre, but even so, the police knew we could not stay at my sister's for long. I kept pointing out that if any of the idiots on the Marquess worked out where we were, my sister and her family would also be in danger. So they eventually put us in a safe house and our furniture in storage.

We had nothing – no furniture, not even a blanket to keep the kids warm, just what we could get in the car. We lived quite a while (about two and a half months) with no furniture and two kids in the little cottage built into the side of a hill and almost in a pub car park. I began to feel safer and mused that maybe the council would let us stay here permanently.

One day we ventured out into the pub garden for a drink. Marc went in and got a drink as I sat staring at Rory and Roisin sleeping (the low window afforded a view of both of them sleeping in the plastic pen we had bought with us and nicknamed 'punkatraz'), as if they were going to chuck themselves out of the window. "Relax," Marc said, sensing my anguish. "They're fine!"

I sat looking at the river just across the road, the boats moored on the island across a few yards of water, which was lapping lazily against them, and the ducks and swans who looked at the tourists offering bread with a kind of cavalier attitude ("Well if you insist, I'll have some of your bread..."), and the wispy willow trees bending in the breeze. I had not experienced such tranquillity for some time. That few moments outside the pub gave me a glimpse of normality again.

Suddenly it began to rain, and as the clouds burst my panic resumed and I rushed back to make sure the kids were OK (not a murmur)! The 'safe house' was also situated next to a church and some of the locals disapproved of my husband's taste in music (and said so), so he would play 'Carmina Burana' loudly as he came out by the church. The occasional intellectual from the pub would get the joke, but these were few and far between. The rest of the populous were bemused by this incomer playing classical music. However, the pub was run by a wonderful woman, who liked showing her tits and had a reputation for sunbathing naked. We had an altercation over the draymen being in the way of me getting to work, and although it was probably a draw, I have admired her feisty attitude ever since. An interesting rebel who speaks her mind, a person of character. She was a proper guv'nor of the old school, and the pub was a nice old country pub – red carpets and discreet lighting, not ruined by some empty suit in a holding company who thinks they're arty. Although a little male dominated (parts of Norfolk are still old fashioned in that way unfortunately), the atmosphere was warm.

Travelling to Yarmouth every day was a bit of a bind. We would have to bathe and dress the kids, and we would all get in the car, Marc being the only driver, and I needed to be there early to prepare for what was still, after all, a stressful and demanding job in itself, without all the other shit we were dealing with. It may not have been violent nutcases banging their fists on the table, but I upset quite a few rural folk before I tempered my interviews to suit a culture that could not deal with my 'in your face' London style.

My colleagues liked to wind me up with the cultural differences, so when they said "Oh dear – you've got the incest family!" I did not take a lot of notice. When they arrived, the young girl said "This is my Dad, and this is our daughter!"

Trying not to look slightly taken aback, I said "Please run this past me again!"

Well I had been warned, but I did not think the old jokes about Norfolk had any basis in truth!

Moving from London in a great hurry caused us a lot of financial hardship. Marc had been working as a self-employed courier. Living without inner London comforts was OK if you are living in Norfolk, but we still had huge debts in London, and with only one of us working now (we daren't leave the kids with anyone else at the time, just in case the criminals found us), the petrol for eighty miles a day was crippling. In London I had used public transport or mostly my push bike. When the car broke down I had to get the train the twenty miles to Yarmouth, instead of three to Camden. Of course being a city girl I absolutely loved the journey – the colleagues travelling with me to Yarmouth Jobcentre were not so enamoured by the countryside as I...

"He was absolutely gorgeous! So what did he say to you?"

"Oooh look, a heron!"

"Yes, Sabena, we know it's a bloody heron! Now, what did he say to you?"

I was determined to bridge the cultural gap, so I went to talk to some share fishermen and arranged a visit to the fields to watch the workers plant seeds by hand and weed the crops. My colleague for some inexplicable reason wore high heels instead of welly boots. "I bloody hate the countryside!" she said in her accent from the wildest most rural part of Norfolk. The irony tickled me pink.

My kids were very obviously from London. When we first took Roisin to a place where kids could get close to real animals (not something you could do in Islington then), she nervously stroked a pot-bellied pig, appeasing him with an "Awight mate?"

On the Norwich market, a policeman ruffled her hair once (she did not take kindly to this for a start). "Hello, and what's your name little girl?" he said.

"I'm not allowed to speak to strangers!" she said scathingly.

"But I'm not a stranger!" he persisted. "I'm a policeman!"

"Ah yes!" she interjected. "But how do I know if you're a nice policeman or a nasty policeman?"

After a moment, and unable to think of an answer, he went off silently to find a local kid who knew the rules! Later Rory (at about the same age) did something similar. He was walking with Marc up a narrow Tudor street in the city centre and coming towards them was a young man who looked as though he had fallen on hard times.

"Is he drunk, Daddy?" he asked at the top of his voice.

"Yes, he is a bit," Marc replied, rather more quietly, and to the amusement of an elderly couple looking in a shop window.

"He's a bit smelly as well Daddy!" Rory continued as the man came within earshot and the couple stifled their laughter.

"Yes, he is a bit!" said Marc, still trying to be tactful.

"Is that what you call a tosser then Daddy?" persisted the wide-eyed boy, as the man passed and the couple looked as though they were going to wet themselves.

"Yes, I expect he probably is!" conceded his dad.

Very fortunately, after a couple of months of barracking the local council, I decided that without being given the opportunity to explain our predicament, I was going to get nowhere fast. I knew our time at the cottage was coming to an end and expected to be re-housed on the city's worst estate. So we went to have a look. Not only was it OK, but Marc and I joked that if we had really been criminals, we could have been 'running the place' by next week.

So I picked someone sympathetic at the council to confide in, expecting to have to agree a move to somewhere horrendous, but she happened to be an ex-policewoman and sorted us out the house we still live in. We went and had a look and asked to move in that day. The council wanted to make it 'habitable', but we said we'd sort that out ourselves if they just let us move in. So that was the end of our stay at the 'safe house'.

The lady next door was a single parent, who worked in the pub, and was very much part of the local community. Her son, James, was also a person of character, who has dealt with some serious problems over the years. Not least of which were some severe learning difficulties. He was however, although a little older, a great influence on our kids, who had been thrust from their familiar surroundings and knew no-one in this new environment. He befriended them without judgement.

Later on the neighbour lent us a bradawl to prop open the window as the sash was broken, and all people could see was the large nose of our big tripe hound Murphy. I will never forget the day we arrived cold, hungry and terrified, to a sparse empty place. The police had told us not to trust anybody. Fortunately, we trusted the lady next door. We told her what had happened, and she just asked us if we needed anything. I think she was quite taken aback when we asked if she had any spare blankets for the kids. But more about her later. We have been the best of friends for over twenty years.

CHAPTER TWELVE
Italian Holiday

This was Marc's third visit to Italy, the first being with his Mum and Dad. They stayed in his Godfather's house in Motta Baluffi. He was eight years old. Six years ago we wrote to Pylade (he had been sending us nougat made locally every Christmas) to tell him we would like to come and visit him in the wilds of Italy. He had been Professor of Italian at the Sorbonne where Marc's father Philip was also teaching. They had formed a lifelong friendship and he had become Marc's Godfather.

When we arrived we were treated like royalty. We had enjoyed it so much we decided to return. Sadly Pylade died before we could save up the money. This short story (to be included as a chapter in my book) is dedicated to Professore Pylade Serafini, a man I am honoured to have met.

Day 1

When we discovered my mobility scooter's smashed up battery on the luggage carousel at Milan airport I thought my holiday had been ruined. I explained that I could only walk a few steps without pain and there was no way I could get a bus, train and taxi to a tiny village outside Cremona by lunchtime without it. My mood went from anger to tears of despair. I felt so helpless. Sometimes disability makes you feel like a baby who can't do anything for themselves.

After I put on my parts, a very overworked but kind airline rep eventually agreed pay the taxi fare to get us there. We arrived at the beautiful bed and breakfast, cum farm, cum museum, and were greeted like old friends by the family Fandani. As promised by Grace (Mariagrazia), Pylade's brother Paolo arrived later and tearfully greeted Marc and I. Louisa cooked us all a delicious spaghetti carbonara, with meat and veg and salad as a second course (as is traditional here). Marc and Louisa gabbled away with each other like long-lost friends, in bits of English, bits of Italian and lots of French, interspersed with appropriate translations for Paolo and Jean-Franco and myself into Italian and English respectively. There was some nice local wine (this is Lambrusco country – nothing like the gnat's piss they export).

The next day we had homemade tortellini, stuffed with ricotta and spinach, ham with herbs and aubergine (this from a woman who says she does not like cooking). There is cake with every meal, even breakfast, so the diet went out the window. In the evening we went for a walk hoping to reach a pizzeria we had been to with Pylade. It was further than we thought and so we dare not risk it in case the battery conked out, so we went back to the local café, where we were treated at first with slight suspicion.

The barista spoke a little English, and asked us politely what the hell English tourists are doing out in the middle of nowhere. Marc's explanation seemed to put everyone at ease and she and the other locals suddenly can't do enough for us. They wanted to know how Marc became Pylade's Godson and where we were staying. Marc's picture in an English magazine sitting on his trike helped. After a couple of hours the barista is taking me by the arm to the ladies' and then sends her boyfriend out for some pizza for us, which she won't let us pay for. I'm going to miss this place!

Day 2

After some expertise was applied by Jean-Franco, who set up the charger so it worked without a British conversion plug, and some discussion by the two expert artisans in how to fix it, it was decided the scooter situation could be better dealt with at Paolo's workshop (before he got any more mastic on Louisa's tablecloth).

Paolo's 'bottega' (workshop) is a wonderful place that has stood still in time, since it was started by Papa Serafini to subsidise the family income, presumably sometime in the 1930's. Leaning against the rough walls of what seems like a two-roomed aircraft hangar, every conceivable size of wood imaginable could be found, from what looked like railway sleepers, to model aeroplane size bits of balsa. In the first room was a huge array of tools, hanging from every space on the walls, neatly categorised according to their function and size. Wood machinery and benches with varying clamps, dotted around the floor in no particular order, ranged from the small and delicate to the heavy and daunting. They were all made of cast iron electrical kit such as drills and lathes. Then there was a huge selection of varnishes, paints, glues, etc.. I would imagine most of these had been considered obsolete for some time by modern day bench joiners. There were several wooden trestles with violin shaped pieces of wood in different stages, up to the finished article on which sat a corkscrew with a mechanism for opening the wine. Paolo showed us one that has been beautifully finished and varnished distinctly in the shape of a Stradivarius, for which the area is famous. These were more local art souvenirs of Cremona than practical bottle openers.

In one corner was a large 'Aga' type stove with a pipe that takes the heat out through the gable end of the roof. It had blatantly been there from the beginning of time. On it were various cooking pots, some containing glue and, curiously, a tomato box containing grapes being dried as raisins. While I was writing he produced various things of beauty from cupboards on the walls. There were a set of differently shaped vases, so perfectly finished and varnished I thought they were glazed ceramics at first. It was only when I picked one up I realised it had been lovingly fashioned from wood. When I explained I thought they were pottery, he produced a mask and a crocodile that are actually terracotta.

There were also various religious icons carved in the shape of a cross, with painted glass and a space in the centre for a Saint or the Madonna. There was also a decorative boomerang (presumably a commission) and an older, dusty model of a big Italian house complete with Juliet style balcony, and a perfect miniature grand piano that worked (the family were still making dolls houses and miniature instruments commercially when Marc first met them in 1968).

Nearby was a pretty still life (presumably another artform Paolo indulged in). Then from another dusty old cupboard he produced the piece de resistance – a raised picture of a rural barn all made of wood, with wagon wheels and old fashioned tools hanging on the wall. There was a yoke, a scythe, a rake and many I didn't recognise, all in miniature and perfect. He gave Marc a nicely crafted little bell that rings.

In one corner of the room was an old 70's television and a chair at a table with a cloth on it, with a half-read newspaper and a coffee cup. They then turned to my battery. Somehow the communication between them was good despite knowing only smatterings of each other's language. They bonded very well over the task in hand, and made a good team. They repaired the casing with the mastic and some electrical tape and glued back the handle. They decided to leave it for three hours while we went back to have a siesta. I was relieved that the sad death of his brother was no longer mentioned and Marc and Paolo were able to continue their friendship without too many painful reminders. After siesta Paolo returned and he and Marc went back to spend some time together at the bottega.

Jean-Franco, Louisa and their daughter Cristina (who I had been in contact with on social media since our last visit, and who had returned from work at the family's factory she now runs) sat around the big table with us in the centre of the huge courtyard. We were joined by 'Le Swisse'. That is, another Cristina who speaks about ten languages, including French and English, who translated so fast that she found herself looking at Marc and I and translating into Italian by mistake. There was also her husband Bruno, who was in fact Swiss (his wife had been born in the village), and who spoke German, French and a lot more Italian than we did. They had bought a house nearby and Bruno intended to retire soon and stay in the village. After the gorgeous dinner Louisa's friend Maurice arrived. He was a gregarious man with a great sense of humour. He used to be a taxi driver, and offered to take us to Milan for 'mate's rates' to save us risking the scooter breaking down on the way to the airport. He came with his wife and another friend (we soon realised that Louisa and Jean-Franco were very popular and people were in and out of the place constantly swapping favours). The wine was flowing and I was able to follow most of the stories and blurt out the occasional phrase in beginner's Italian and fractured French.

After they had gone, a storm began brewing – there was thunder and lightning (although no rain at this point). This involved taking everything indoors except the table and chairs, in case the area under the marquee was flooded. I was assured all the animals (including the rabbits) would be fine.

The noisy menagerie started their pandemonium at about four in the morning. The goats seemed to be the main conspirators of the racket. They would start bleating in the ear of the head goose (named Picora), who would start the others off. Then the sheep (in a separate enclosure) joined in, then the ducks and then eventually the head cockerel would wake up and start giving it large. The hens would cackle and by four thirty there was enough noise to wake the dead. Not that it bothered me – I loved it.

Day 3

With my battery fixed as well as it could be, I felt confident enough to trundle to the local café again (just around the corner). Word had got round and everyone seemed to know all about us and Marc's connection to the legendary Professore, who had introduced his English Godson to everyone so proudly on our last visit. We went back and had our breakfast and waited for Paolo's return. When he arrived I knew he was with Mariagrazia as Franco pointed out her car. She was her usual effervescent and excitable self. It was great to see her in person again, and her trip to India seemed to have left her in rude health. She was wearing Indian style clothes which suited her well and she and Paolo seemed more relaxed in each other's company. Perhaps they had become closer in their united grief for the person they both loved best in the world.

We went to a splendid restaurant and had a gastronomic lunch. "I'm a vegetarian," she said as she tucked into a piece of veal, of a sort that would be banned in England for humanitarian reasons. "At least, in India I'm vegetarian, but here it is impossible!"

I had to agree with her that any kind of diet was difficult out in the Italian countryside. Mariagrazia's zest for life is contagious and Marc and I enjoy being in her company. Not to mention her language expertise, and with Paolo's laidback charm, they complimented each other's personality well. She spoke about her work in India and her disappointment in the way people she thought she could trust used their 'spirituality' to gain money. It occurred to me that the legacy of Pylade's and Philip's friendship had left us in the company of people we could trust.

In the evening, Louisa heated some pizza we bought at the shop for us, and she still spoilt us with some wine from her kitchen to go with it. Louisa and Marc continued talking in French, Italian and English. Franco and I were concentrating hard to keep up. Franco had promised to show us the other museum. We had already been shown the astonishing collections of rocks and animal remains from the River Po, including coral and huge ammonites, behind one part of the central courtyard. He was, as usual, off doing something on his forklift but had left the door open so we entered carefully. This was another experience, a world of barrel organs and old gramophones, music boxes and automatons. Looking was one thing, but Franco caught up with us and ran from exhibit to exhibit like an excited child, turning them on and explaining them in bits of English, French and charade, transporting us to times gone by. For me it evoked childhood experiences in London of costermongers with monkeys who collected money and my Nan's music boxes, and similar automatons owned by my family, of singing drunks holding up lamp-posts. The noise was fantastic! At the end of the room was his 'piece de resistance'. It was a full-sized fairground organ with a band that played their instruments on the front. An audible and visual delight – I'm glad we did not miss it.

Day 4

In addition to agreeing to take us to Milan, Maurice had kindly offered to take us to Cremona to change some money. He arrived early, they loaded the scooter and in no time we were back, looking at the sun-blushed fields. Maurice pointed out the buildings and explained that most were making bio-fuel, although there still seemed to be plenty of cattle, tomatoes and wheat – spaghetti bolognese as far as the eye could see.

After six banks we gave up trying to change travel money. Maurice was great company, with a wicked sense of humour, not to mention patience (they had to keep lifting my scooter up and down steps). After getting some souvenirs in the sprawling market (the usual mixture of tat and interesting bargains), and some successful cockney-style bartering from me, we found the shop that sold miniature violins Marc wanted, with a back room that resembled a museum.

We drank coffee near the Duomo (Cremona's statuesque cathedral) that dominates the historic square. Later, after a nice lunch in a posh restaurant (more sumptuous pasta and tasty wine), Maurice took us back. I love the countryside anywhere, but I would swap it for noise and people any day.

In the evening two friends I had not seen before turned up with a 4x4 full of hunting dogs, and they also brought the biggest rooster out of the back by the feet, which were tied up with string. I assumed he was for eating, until I realised he was very much alive. Apparently he was going to quieten the other lot down at night somehow.

Day 5

We were ready and pensive at eight. Louisa and Franco had a flat in the mountains they needed to check on and had invited us along. The journey took us past the fields and flat terracotta and yellow houses, to ones with more age and character, with ornate shutters and balconies. We stopped to take photos above Lake Garda, where the sun was the most 'mad dogs and Englishmen'.

Although the village at our destination was distinctly alpine, like the one in France where Marc's sister Sophie got married, it was also reminiscent of Trudos in Cyprus. There were gardens and olive groves built on rocky outcrops and church spires balanced tentatively on the peaks. The flat was small and compact (the only thing you could equate with a London council flat). It was modern but very Mediterranean and did not look out of place in the picturesque village. After a look round (and a lot of posing for photos), and trying to convince yet another bank we were not the Brink's-Mat Robbers, we ate in the back garden of a large restaurant, next to a small but unused swimming pool. Shockingly Marc swapped with me for a pasta covered in Gorgonzola (never seen him eat blue cheese of any sort before), and left me with the best homemade gnocchi I have ever tasted (lots of sage, spinach and ricotta). None of the restaurants called pizzerias mentioned pizza once – must just be for tourists.

On our return Louisa treated us to yet another nice home cooked pasta and more wine – well it would be rude not to, as they say in Norfolk!

Day 6

Mariagrazia arrived at eleven and stopped off in Cremona to pick up a beautifully wrapped package, that I later found out contained the most exquisite, aesthetically pleasing little cakes (diet next week), that we had after dinner with one of her neighbour's creations that tasted like cinnamon cake. After a visit to the pharmacy and fiddling with her verruca, we went to her beautiful house near Parma. We had a great lunch under the ash tree, in her walnut grove with, and assisted by two splendid neighbours, who were full of fun and character. Mariagrazia's brother turned up, who also spoke English so we all knew what was occurring. She had to do something essential in the evening (something to do with publishing Pylade's poems I think), so Paolo kindly came and took us home.

On the way, he took us to the house he had shared with his brother to show us a picture. It was an early one of Marc's Mum's (signed only June) of a local ornate gatehouse to an old monastery. Marc remembers her painting it from a picture. The dramatic image looks as though it is in a storm and it was dated 1969, the year after they visited. As it was just up the road from the house Paolo stopped outside the building. It was an emotional experience and all three of us were close to tears.

Back in the courtyard, Maurice and his wife turned up with a pot full of what was apparently wild boar sauce to go with pasta, and we had a big farewell party for 'les Engleesh'. After dinner Emanuel turned up with a delicious chocolate and vanilla pudding made by his mother (Marc asked him if she would care to adopt a hairy Englishman), and Cristina came out of the kitchen with some very Italian ice-cream. Franco opened a huge bottle of Prosecco, and a good time was had by all.

I hope that our wonderful holiday served to endorse not only the lifelong friendship between Philip and Pylade and their days at the Sorbonne, together with June's extraordinary talent, but also our relationship with Motta Balluffi and Torricella del Pizzo.

CHAPTER THIRTEEN
Broads Minded

The general populous in our area asserted that incomers needed a passport to live in Norwich. It was rumoured locally that we received ours quite quickly, due to the fact that we were scary. So the customary shy nod, usually afforded foreigners, might not be sufficient acknowledgement. Of course the more open minded people in 'Peasant Crescent' (as Marc dubbed our street) ignored all the rumours of "They must be drug dealers!" or "You don't go on witness protection unless you've got wrong!", and found out in conversation with us that we were blatantly neither of these things. We had just been in the wrong place at the wrong time.

Irritating as the gossip was, at first it kept the idiots at bay. Some people are still hiding behind an inability to admit they were wrong. In fact some of the local numpties have not bothered to get to know us in twenty years. Even twenty years later, occasionally you can see the little lightbulb above the head of some would-be bumpkin slowly flicker on. The husband said some are so daft that they have skid-marks on their forehead, because so many conversations keep going over their head.

Even a decade later, when Marc was a shorthand writer at the Crown Court and I was working with the police signing people on at the probation office, people were still talking about us as the new Bonnie and Clyde! I must point out that this is a minority of the local folk, who are the exception that proves the rule. The majority of people know here are intelligent beings who are not living testament to the film 'Deliverance'.

In the early days, the landlord and lady of the nearest pub to 'Peasant Crescent' retired, and the new one, John, and I became mates and sat talking for hours after time. He was an intelligent man and he became my confidant and friend. Of course the local gossip-mongerers thought there was more to our relationship. I had not yet realised men and women were not allowed to be mates in these parts. I had no reason or desire to mess about with anyone else! As they say, and no offence to John, but why go out for a hamburger if you've got steak at home?

Customers (who were almost all men) in the local pubs did not particularly like women propping up the bar, especially women with an opinion who were used to conversing with men as an equal. But I did meet some nice people in the local pubs, including John's ex-wife Sue and her husband Eddie, who both worked for him. There was also Babs who was smashing company – loads of laughs and loved her brandy, as well as her boys, who I got to know later. When she got old and infirm I used to go and visit her at her care home. Some days she would say "How are you, how's the family?", and so on. The next time she would say "Who are you?"

I hope if my marbles go a bit, people will still come and keep me company!

I especially enjoyed the company of our lovely friend Rodney. Rodney and I got pissed together for about three weeks before I understood what he was on about. Deciphering accents is not something Norfolk people are renowned for either, so, bright as he was, I'm sure whatever rubbish I was clattering on about drunkenly in my cockney got missed quite a bit. Mind you, talking bollocks when you're wankered is what you go to the pub for.

Eventually he told me all about his sons and Jenny, his wife and her family, and I began to understand the man. Not only his accent, but also where he was coming from. He was a laugh, for instance – he once got a cab from the pub to take him home to his farm (it was just across the road). Neither of us lived a spit away from the pub, but I've carried him home and he I on several occasions.

Marc's first real conversation with Rodney was much more interesting. Marc had been working at a local slaughterhouse. The lads working there were all brawn and no necks. Bizarrely, there was this constant whine of country & western music to calm the pigs (apparently sheep and cattle are not so bright, but pigs are intelligent and often predict their own demise – mind you, if anyone started playing me country & western I would probably think I was approaching the 'Pearly Gates').

After two weeks of this back-breaking work (Marc's a strong man, but you needed to be built like two brick shithouses tied together), and an award for long service (a packet of fags), he'd had enough and plonked himself in the local.

Rodney said, "You look a bit down chap... what's the matter?"

Marc proceeded to tell him about this awful man he worked for at an abattoir, near Great Yarmouth (which was 20 miles away from there, and anywhere else), and how he was a slave driver, as well as rude and expecting too much of his workers. Rodney looked pensive for a moment and then said, "I quite agree with everything you've said, he's my brother in law!"

Only in Norfolk!

For a long time we would get meat from Rodney in exchange for favours. We would go Sunday morning to the lovely little small-holding. He kept his meat in a small cold-store out the back in one of the myriad barns that were left over from a time long forgotten. The kids and I would help feed the cattle. Jenny would make me a cup of tea (I rarely drink tea, but hers was special). I used to enjoy those Sunday mornings. Marc was commissioned to paint a lovely picture of the farm, which still has pride of place on the wall. Sadly, Rodney died of cancer recently – a great loss to his family, the local community, Marc and myself.

Marc told me about other incidents at the slaughterhouse. One bloke came to work with a dreadful hangover, and threw up on the floor. Marc was a little taken aback at the phrase "You dirty bastard!" as he was covered in blood and viscera and the floor was about to be washed and re-strawed after the pigs. Marc had also made the mistake of saying he had some friends in the next village (Limpenhoe). This was not received well, and his colleagues broke into an embarrassed silence until one bloke explained without a smidgen of tongue in cheek, "We don't talk to them, they're all inbred – isn't that right Cousin Charlie, Uncle Fred, etc.?"

In fact all five of his relations agreed!

On our first visit to the now notorious Prince of Wales Road (Norwich's 'Clubland'), we stood waiting to be searched when a bouncer beckoned us in. He said, "Alright you two, come in – what are you waiting for?"

When we explained, he said Norwich will never be as bad as London – "We don't have to search people here!"

He was absolutely right, and indeed there have been some perfectly respectable clubs there – one of Marc's biker friends used to own one. The rumours my husband put about, that later in another club I took the piss out of a much larger bouncer (I knew him anyway and had got him the job), were grossly exaggerated. And if I did turn to his mate and say, "And as for you, you long streak of piss...!" – I was drunk at the time (Your Honour), and I don't remember.

The bouncers loved the fact that we were not scared of anyone and stood for no nonsense, but we were not really badly behaved either, and we never had trouble getting in anywhere. We got suited and booted and went to a lovely pub, just off the Norwich market. We sat at one end of the bar and the rest of the customers sat on the other, with a huge gap in between, even though it was busy. Some brave people came and chatted to us eventually, but we still don't know if they thought we were police or thieves!

There were so few people of colour in Norwich, especially twenty years ago, that being black or even of mixed lineage in Norfolk was like being a member of a club. Marc and I saw a reggae band advertised, although the name would have been a bit crass for London (and they were all getting on a bit), but they were good. We decided to have a look, especially as people warned us about the pub being rough. We were suited and booted and again made people nervous. People panicked as soon as we turned up and started emptying their pockets on the floor, until someone recognised us. Although most of the audience were white, the few people of colour we knew, from all different places in Norwich, all seemed to be at the same gig.

John had a little business doing coach trips. The coaches were parked behind the pub. Shockingly, he had a terrible accident. I'm not sure exactly what happened – I know the barman who found him was very upset. It seems he got squashed by one of the coaches and died despite the Air Ambulance's prompt arrival. Marc and I were very sad.

The local was taken over by John's son, with whom I did not particularly get on. His dad once said to him, "You want to listen to her, she's run a pub!"

From that moment he seemed to dislike me. One of his favourite customers and his missus were in there one night and they took exception to me not being a racist out of the dark ages like them. So we had a heated political argument (how dare a women have a point of view). When I next walked in the pub, the resident 'usual suspects' gave me a round of applause.

He gave me some sort of grief. I apologised for having a point of view, being the diplomatic person I am and thought that was an end to it. But then there was another time when I stood up to one of his thugs (who was trying to tell me where I could sit and who I could talk to). We did not care to go in after that, but about a year later I popped in one lunchtime and he told me I was barred (the only pub I've ever been barred from).

So I started drinking in the pub next to the safe house. Unfortunately, the new managers (who were lovely) had to put up with his racist mate and his missus (who told me and another woman on the bus that he beat her up), as they were friends with the landlady's dad. Just to illustrate the extent of the stupidity of the few remaining ill-educated twats in the local community – he sacked his daughter and son-in-law, who were good managers who had made something of the place, and gave this idiot the pub to run with his money.

Apart from rumours of overt racism (they had a 'gollywog' on the bar to illustrate to customers who they wanted to keep out,) and some décor ideas that only a self-important incompetent would go ahead with – like putting paving stones on the bar floor that were so 'on the wonk', to use a Norfolk expression, that you thought you were pissed before you started drinking – he gave him the pub to run and he made such an impossible mess of it before he drunk himself to death that he alienated all the customers and lifted everything he could take with him.

John's son managed to do pretty much the same trick in the other pub and is now hiding from his creditors. What's all this crap got to do with me, you might ask? Well you see, apart from the lack of a decent local pub, there was also the fact that a certain element of the local police had decided that being on the witness protection scheme must mean you are a criminal. You would think we had suffered enough grief but this judgemental attitude had excluded us from the usual security you would expect society to bestow upon a vulnerable family who had chosen to do the right thing. It left us in a situation where any Tom, Dick or Harry who bullied us, however criminal, could be sure the police would take their side.

For instance, when the thug threw me on the floor because I would not do as I was told, or when Marc was three sheets to the wind on Christmas Eve, and three idiots of the same family kicked him around a car-park for no reason (he still had their boot marks on his clothes), nothing was done. When the racist manager objected to Marc slowing down outside his pub (we were not daft enough to go in there) and chased him home getting out of the car with a big knife, nothing was done. However, when Marc got out of the car saying, "Come on then sunshine, I don't know what your problem is, but let's have it out!" the imbecile got straight back in his car and fucked off! In all these cases the police took the side of the perpetrators. The worst example of this of this was when we were in Oz.

When my lovely Dad died he left us all a bit of money (me, my sister and Shaun who I grew up with, who always looked after my parents and still looks after Mum by doing odd jobs for her).

Anyway, Budgie, my Aussie friend and I had always kept in touch (we worked together for Guvvy, up the Passage). So I rang her and asked if she could recommend any hotels in Perth because we wanted to come for a holiday. She said her sister would be away so she would stay at her place and we could live at hers. I thought we were talking about a flat. When we got there it was this huge big beautiful house. I introduced my family and then we started chatting about old times. After about half an hour, Marc remarked that we had not seen each other for twenty-two years and we spoke to each other as if talked to each other yesterday!

(We have lost touch recently but I am hoping she will reappear after emerging from some exotic country – she once said to me something like "The world's population is 7.4 billion people and I have not met half of them!").

After our wonderful holiday of a lifetime we got back to find the police had busted the door down as John's son had told them we had abandoned the dog. My friend Kerry, who was looking after Murphy (her and her sons were taking him for walks twice a day and making sure he had food and water) had to go and get him back from the dog pound on the bus (she does not drive either). He was old and this piece of nastiness could have killed him. They were suitably apologetic and paid for the damage, but everything had been thoroughly searched – whatever they thought we had hidden obviously was not there.

In addition to the big fence around the house and the trees (Marc and I were sitting in the garden on a sunny day talking about having little dreams, he said I would like to plant some big trees at the front to cut out the traffic noise – I can't look at them now without remembering that idyllic little afternoon), Marc built a huge wooden shed to do his art in. It was the venue for some outrageous local parties, and some really happy times. My friend Sam, who I worked with in Clapton Youth Centre, brought a steel band to attend a cavalcade in Yarmouth at about this time. It came as quite a shock to a place that equality and diversity seemed to have passed by.

When they were little, Roisin was a terrible tell-tale, and much more sneaky than Rory. I had managed to grow some strawberries in the garden (this was unusual for me – I'm prone to murdering plants, apparently you are supposed to water them and stuff). There was one left, which she wiped round his face and then grassed him up (she did not eat fruit).

"Muuuuum! Wowy's nicked a stwawbewy!"

She was scuppered as he could not have reached some bits of himself that were strawberry coloured. She did the same another time, dropping bits of his banana all over the kitchen.

"Look! Wowy's made a mess with his badada!"

When we lived in the safe house behind the pub we had hook-and-eyes on the doors to stop the kids wandering if we left the room. Rory would lie down and Roisin would stand on him, finding something to credit-card the door open. This was a trick she learned when we were on our 'honeymoon' in Spain. My parents had a place in near Malaga, so we stayed there with them and took the kids (maybe not everyone's idea of a honeymoon but we had a great time). The front gate had a latch little madam had learned to open in the same way.

We took the kids all over the place, taking advantage of our access to so much rural education. Having said that, education in Norwich still seems poor and jaded in comparison with the 'make it happen' attitude sported by London's learning culture. Although our kids had some wonderfully inspired teachers, it would seem not many working class kids are very ambitious in Norfolk. I don't know if it is leftover from a forelock touching class system. As with other parts of the country, the kids with unhappy and unambitious parents are the least interested. With this goes a strange snobbery I have never encountered anywhere else I have spent time. Most of it perpetrated, it would appear, by the people who had the least to offer! It was not until I came here that I really believed people would dislike you for living in a council house. In London, you've got to be a millionaire to live in a house, council or otherwise.

Rory, being a bright lad but sensitive, was bullied mercilessly by the kids in his class. He would also be the one who was caught retaliating, after being goaded by much more sneaky individuals. The head teacher eventually agreed to put him down a class after Marc persuaded him it was in Rory's best interest. Of course anything was better than him coming home upset every day, and having his work affected. After the move he never looked back. But it left him in a class of kids who had no ambition or desire to learn, and that made it difficult for us to help.

Roisin got bullied as well but she was a little more resilient. Little as she was, she gave one kid a right good hiding for trying to bully her brother. The teacher, Marc and I found it hard to punish this piece of bravery, so we all just gave her a "Violence isn't the answer!" type lecture and left it at that.

Generations of students have left the local high school and college having learned as little as they expected from a place that seems to have been left behind educationally by successive governments. Roisin finished her Travel & Tourism course at college, and Rory his Carpentry. Neither had much to do with their present jobs but all education is good.

On a better note we took the kids to Marc's sister's wedding in France among the Alps. The place was beautiful and it was nice spending some time with June and Marc's 'Auntie' Jean and Paolo, our nephew – despite the bad behaviour and meanness of Marc's only rich relations (you would not believe they were related to lovely, generous, socialist Philip).

Sadly the marriage did not work out, but I hope one day to meet Paolo's younger brother Scott. We also visited my long-time friend Philippa in Roosky in the heart of

Ireland when she lived there (her ex-husband Robin, a well-known violinist, who was in the Balham Alligators and their daughter Rosie, a musician herself, discovered Roisin had a flair for the piano).

We also took a trip to see another good friend from London, Annie, in her native Northumberland (I had never been before), as well as Marc's Dutch 'Auntie' Jonneke in Amsterdam.

Last but not least, we visited Marc's lovely godfather – an Oxford Don, who taught at the Sorbonne with Marc's dad (rather than a member of the Mafia). So it's fair to say my kids have been able to travel a bit and have had an opportunity for some cultural understanding.

We went back to London when Mike Khan married Dee (her parents wrote 'Thunderbirds', which she and her mum had just finished writing a new series of when she sadly lost her). I had also known Dee for quite a long time and was ecstatic when they got married. Despite her privileged upbringing Dee is a kind and down to earth person, who is interested in people's goodness rather than status, and an amazingly talented singer to boot! It was fabulous to see all my good London mates and I'm glad Mike and Dee had some good times before his heart problem finally got him. He leaves behind some of the best songs ever written.

At that difficult age, Roisin was having some problems (some of which I don't wish to cover). She had befriended a girl at school who had a lot more problems, saying she felt sorry for her. Anyway her stupid or nasty mother (I have not decided which yet, as long as I never have to meet her, things will be fine) decided to kidnap Roisin with some kind of Christian conversion as an ulterior motive. This dangerous woman persuaded Roisin to tell the authorities that we beat her, and turned up one day to take her clothes asserting herself as Roisin's rescuer. Marc was asleep when Roisin used her key, although he called the police immediately – he did not want to give this evil woman any more fuel. By the time they turned up, she and Roisin had gone. Needless to say the police were completely uninterested in helping us get back a vulnerable sixteen year old from a religious nutter. They did assure me that neither they nor the authorities had believed we beat her.

How complicit Roisin was in this arrangement I have never been sure, but I use the word 'kidnap' advisedly, as we were not estranged (although she told the Jobcentre we were apparently, not that my very professional colleague would have disclosed that information). Eventually, on the verge of a nervous breakdown, I spoke to my very sensible and caring sister, who persuaded Roisin to meet at McDonald's, where she helped us talk things through and Roisin returned. I know that's what sisters do but I will always be grateful – I thought I had lost my daughter forever.

In addition to Debbie, our first friend here, another fine example of intelligent Norfolk is the lovely Kerry! We had been here quite a long time before I got friendly with Kerry, although she only lived round the corner. Her three went to the same schools (not a lot of choice around here). She and I would get drunk round her house and play records (for people who have not encountered these – they were round bits of vinyl that made a noise a bit like CDs). Kerry's company was partly responsible for stopping me getting hazardously drunk in the local pubs. Marc and I could rarely afford babysitters, so were used to going out alone. She even took the kids to school for us so we could both work for a while. This was the birth of the locally renowned 'Witchy Wednesday' (so called by Marc as he reckons he has to turn up the telly because of the cackling, and that all the women present were scary).

When Kerry told my colleagues that she wanted a job as soon as her youngest was in high school they were sceptical (lots of people say that). However, she did an office course and got a job in the NHS as planned. At first she was a little under confident. One day a couple of months into her job she said, "Who could have guessed a year ago that I would be working full time in a good job!"

Marc and I yelled in unison, "We did!"

Now when she does an interview for a sideways move and some dopey manager asks her what job she wants to end up with, she says "Yours!"

Although I struggled with Norwich at first, because it had many of the elements I hated about Teddington, it has afforded me the experience of a much more courteous community whose lack of enthusiasm may be frustrating, but the lack of confrontation will probably help me live longer. My job allowed me to gain a measure understanding of local culture, ethos and humour. Especially running a little office up on the huge building site in the city centre and working for a year at the local probation with naughty boys and girls (I may have had a problem with some of my colleagues on the team, but never with the police or probation officers, who were proper professionals).

This had given me a better understanding of the place, and that, more than anything, made me love it enough to make it my home. Although my moral compass may not align with everyone's credo, I am proud of my love for people and hope my humility makes up for my other failings.

I have had a sometimes difficult life, but I have mainly been very happy. It's been an interesting journey, but despite all the good things, somewhere in the back of my mind is an overwhelming sadness and heartache that I never achieved the lifetime acting ambition. Not fame, not money – just to have been able to use my talent to have a done better as an entertainer.

There will always be a bit of me, still on the stage, under the lights, with the audience clapping and cheering...!

Printed in Great Britain
by Amazon